"*Oh My God.*
IT'S ME!"

"*Oh My God.* IT'S ME!"

by

Dr. Sheryl Valentine

White Knight Books
Toronto, Canada

Published in 2006 by
White Knight Books, a division of Bill Belfontaine Ltd.
Suite 103, One Benvenuto Place, Toronto Ontario Canada M4V 2L1
T. 416-925-6458 F. 416-925-4165 • e-mail whitekn@istar.ca
www.whiteknightbooks.ca

Ordering information

CANADA	**UNITED STATES**
White Knight Books	APG Distributors
c/o Georgetown Terminal Warehouses	(Associated Publishers' Group)
34 Armstrong Avenue,	1501 County Hospital Road
Georgetown ON, L7G 4R9	Nashville, TN, 37218 USA
T: 1-866-485-5556 F: 1-866-485-6665	T: 1-888-725-2606 F: 1-800-510-3650

First printing: April 2006

Library and Archives Canada Cataloguing in Publication
Valentine, Sheryl
Oh, my god, it's me! : a valuable blend of inspiration
and spirituality / by Sheryl Valentine.
ISBN 0-9736705-8-4
1. Self-actualization (Psychology)—Religious aspects.
2. Spiritual life. I. Title.
BJ1581.V35 2006   204   C2006-900375-0

Cover Art:
Cover and Text Design: Karen Thomas Petherick
Cover image: © FirstLight.ca
Back Cover Picture: Julie Baumgarten

Printed and Bound in Canada

IN DEDICATION

To: Bill and Bobby.
Words cannot express the
many blessings you have
brought to my life.
I most treasure the gift
of your unconditional love.
I Love You!

ACKNOWLEDGEMENTS

Once a book is published the most visible contributor is the author. However, so many people contributed to this book, and while less visible, without every single one of them this book would not be in your hands.

I feel much gratitude and love for my husband and son: Bill and Bobby. I truly could not have written without them. Nothing has made me so aware of God's presence in my life as the gift of them, to me. I thank them immensely for tolerating the many years of "porch-dwelling" that it took to write this book.

Much love to my mother who always knew I could to it.

In twenty-plus years as a doctor, I have interacted with literally thousands of people. So many of them have shared their lives with me and in one way or another, many of their stories appear in this book. *Thank you*!

I especially want to thank all who have attended my lectures on spirituality over the years, without you this book really could not have been written.

Thank you to Jan Uebersetzig for being not only a supportive friend over many years, but also for teaching me a few things about writing. Thanks to my husband, Marni Anderson and Brisia Gorey for reading this book and offering their insights while it was in process.

In the final stages when I actually thought the book was just about perfect, my publisher, Bill Belfontaine, gave me a rude awakening when he edited my book! I thank him for mentoring me to the next level – from amateur writer to professional.

Thank you to Karen Thomas Petherick who designed the amazing book cover and who turned my manuscript into such a wonderful book.

I am grateful to Julie Baumgarten who took my photo for this book. She captured the essence of who I am and actually made me somewhat photogenic!

This may sound strange, but then again, my book is on spirituality—I actually practice this stuff! While seeking a publisher I thought of God as my agent. I trusted that I would be led to just the right publisher for me and my book. *Thank you* God for a lot of things, but especially for bringing me to …

Bill Belfontaine, founder of White Knight Books, is amazing! *Thank You!* and much love to you Bill for recognizing my gifts, my potential and for turning my dreams into reality—and for being a funny, ethical and inspirational guy to boot!

Last but not least, I want to acknowledge you the reader for picking up this book. I hope you gain as much from reading it as I did from writing it. *Thank you!*

– Dr. Sheryl Valentine

CONTENTS

INTRODUCTION

THIS BOOK IS ABOUT LEARNING TO LIVE CONSCIOUSLY. You are needed in this world. Your true Self yearns to extend itself creatively, abundantly and with love—but cannot do so as long as you remain unconscious of it. Most of us are familiar with the Biblical message: *You shall know the truth and the truth shall set you free.* It's not the truth about a person, place or thing that will set you free. Coming home to the truth about you will set you free.

We all experience reoccurring problems in our relationships, with money, jobs, body issues, and with our emotions. Who is the common denominator in each problem?

When I reflect on the timing of the significant breakthroughs in my life, I can see that they occurred only after I realized: "Oh My God. It's ME!" These five words are life changing. Their very utterance puts out to the universe that you are ready to bring awareness and ownership to the state of your life. In this moment of recognition you may not be aware of what you are doing or just how you are doing it, but awareness that you are doing it will lead to healing.

As long as we think that people and forces outside of us cause our negative circumstances, we cannot effect change. We have been endowed with free will, and thus consciousness is never forced on us. With even the slightest inkling that you contribute to your circumstances, you invite the universe to help you, and will thus be led to the ideas, people and information that will bring you further along your path. Pay attention. Your life will reveal what needs healing in you. With awareness, you will come to know that your Spirit constantly guides you toward consciousness and healing. When you are willing to heal on the inside—lasting change occurs on the outside.

Are you a self-help junkie? So was I. After ten years of a steady diet of self-help material, I actually did help myself. My adventures in self-help led me to the study and practice of spiritual principles where I finally realized that there is no such thing as self-healing. We cannot heal alone. Not only do we need spiritual assistance, we also need each another.

"Oh My God. It's ME!" is a practical book. Knowledge of spiritual principles is useless until we learn to apply them to the practical aspects of daily life. Over the years many people have told me that they don't have time to cultivate a spiritual practice. You don't have time not to. Cultivating a relationship with your Spirit is not a luxury, but a necessity—one that will transform you, and thus create a life where hope becomes reality.

And more than once I've been told, "This spiritual stuff is too hard!" I'm the first to admit that applying spiritual principles to the ins-and-outs of our daily lives is hard work—but it's not "too hard." What's too hard is living our lives in a chronic state of anger, worry, guilt and fear. What's too hard is living without the recognition that the Source of all love, guidance and strength is alive and well within us.

In this book you will find practical solutions for many of life's challenges—as it points to the true Source of healing. Whether struggling through conflicts with relationships, money, jobs, self-worth and the like, it is my hope that you will find inspiration and a solid source of help in the pages of *"Oh My God. It's ME!"*

CLARIFICATION OF TERMS

The spiritual principles set forth in *"Oh My God. It's ME!"* do not adhere to a particular religious affiliation. Since the use of *any* spiritual term is potentially controversial, it is necessary to clarify a few being used throughout this book.

God

When it comes to "God" all language ultimately fails to define the indefinable. As I pondered what I wanted to say here, I came across the following exchange on an online discussion group:

Someone asked: "Without sounding like a mischief maker, may I ask how on earth we can be so certain there is a god/father? I mean, I have run into angels before, but never the big guy in the sky. Is god nature? I don't get it."

Stephen Calder provided the best reply: "Yes, in a sense God *is* nature. God is that within you which is perfect, that which you are part of that is a perfect whole, creating in an instant all creation and you with it, an instant that is always now. It is the eternal and only true reality, and it doesn't matter whether you think of it as all encompassing love, or infinite intelligence, or God or Goddess, or as a person or not. It will always and only be what it *is*, the infinity of being, never changing but ever extending. You're not supposed to get it. Let it get you."

Every attempt has been made to forgo the use of masculine and feminine pronouns in reference to "God." When it could not be avoided, however, the masculine pronoun is used.

Holy Spirit

I do not associate the term "holy spirit" with a religion. It appeals to me because it denotes the presence of a "whole" spirit within that is always in communication with God. Throughout this book, Holy Spirit is used interchangeably with Inner Voice, Inner Spirit, God's Spirit and the Spirit Within.

Ego

"Ego" denotes the small, limited fearful self that believes it is separate from God and from others.

Self

The word "self" spelled with a capital "S" denotes our divine nature as in our true Self.

1 HEALING THROUGH RELATIONSHIPS

*We relate, react and respond
to other people based on how
we feel about ourselves.*

– Sheryl Valentine

_____

*The Holy Spirit's temple is not a
body, but a relationship.*

– A Course in Miracles

LOVE ON PURPOSE

L inus, my favorite "Peanuts" character said, "I love humanity—it's people I can't stand!" A few of us can relate to that. Many years ago, I had a revelation that there is nothing more important than learning how to give and receive love. I made a decision then and there that I was going to figure out this love thing. Since then I have learned quite a bit about love, although I readily admit to being remedial in the practice of it.

Learning to love can be frustrating because while we are often told to love other people, no one tells us how. It was a big turning point when I realized that no one could tell us how to love. Before we can truly love other people and ourselves, we must first bring awareness to why we don't.

A Course in Miracles says that your task is not to seek for love, but merely to seek and find, within yourself, all of the barriers that you have built against it.[1] Therefore, learning how to love requires a willingness to uncover your obstacles to love. All the chapters in this book will be helpful in this regard, but first, it is important to understand the following.

You Cannot Do It by Yourself

Love is God's territory. We are taught how to love through the Spirit of God that lives within us. Most of us walk in the world with the ego leading the way. The ego and the Holy Spirit are not people occupying our minds. Rather, they represent two choices: fear or love. We have really only one choice, however, because fear is almost always on automatic pilot! If we could choose against fear we wouldn't need the Inner Spirit. Not only do we need spiritual assistance, we need each other.

Healing Through Relationships

We are all the same. Each one of us desires appreciation, approval and to love and be loved. Somewhere along the way we have been hurt, betrayed and rejected. And suffered. As a result, we have erected barriers around our heart. These unconscious blocks to love separate us from other people, God and our true Self.

The primary block to love is fear. Our conflicts stem from an unconscious fear of love. Ego = Fear = Separation. When God's Spirit is invited into our relationships, they can be used to reveal our fears and return us home to love. Holy Spirit = Love = Union.

Feelings of negativity toward anyone, from the clerk in a store to your mate are opportunities to seek help and healing: 'Holy Spirit, please help me see this person or situation through your eyes of love rather than mine of judgment and fear.' Your responsibility is to ask for help. Your Spirit takes it from there. Only the loving tutelage of the Inner Teacher can heal you, and thus your relationships. With God's Spirit as your teacher, all relationships become a classroom where you can learn the lessons of love.

LESSON ONE

☙

Love Is a Choice

"Love" is defined as "feeling strong affection for someone or something." Most of us can readily come up with at least a short list of those people or things for which we feel strong affection. But what about this: *Love your enemies.* Most people think that they don't have enemies. An enemy, however, is anyone who even mildly irritates you. Ah—now you have a problem. In the face of irritation, do you feel love? You probably won't feel love unless he or she stops irritating you. And that might not happen either!

Love is not just a feeling. Love is a choice. Love is a practice. Love is something you do on purpose. Understand that the enemy is not outside of you, but resides in your own mind. The ego, being fear, is an adversary to love. But fear, is merely a choice. Bring awareness to the fact that judgmental, fearful or angry thoughts are not love. You can then make another choice.

One morning I was more than *mildly* irritated at my teenage son. While getting ready for work, I thought about the things he had done recently that irked me. Then I realized that my angry and condemning thoughts were not helping anything. And so I prayed: 'Dear God, I surrender my feelings to you, please transform them.' I then thought, 'I love you Bobby, I forgive you and I forgive myself. Together, we receive the blessing of God's love and peace.' Prior to that prayer I wasn't feeling all that loving, but my choice to practice love on purpose brought me back to feeling love.

If you want to learn how to love, then be prepared to pause and do a similar practice several times a day—every day. Let's face it, most of us become mildly irritated at least a few times in a day. When irritated at the person who pulls in front of you on the freeway, the grocery store clerk who is too slow, whoever or whatever, all are opportunities to recognize your hostile opponent to love. It's not that you're not supposed to have unloving thoughts, just none that you would keep. Give your unloving thoughts to the Inner Spirit so that they can be transformed.

༺✖༻

I'm Sorry

These words can bring so much healing into any relationship. I'll admit that sometimes saying "I'm sorry" is a tough one. Before God's Spirit took hold on me "I'm sorry" was not in my vocabulary!

One night, World War III broke out in our living room. I have no idea what my husband and son do after such altercations, but I pray. I ask for Divine help and invariably, through no strength of my own, I find myself saying or doing the right thing. So after this particular war, I used this powerful prayer:

> *Dear God,*
> *I desire healing for myself, that I may share it with*
> *Bill and Bobby, whom I love.*
> *It is not possible that I can have healing without*
> *them, or they without me.*
> *Yet it is wholly possible for us to share it now.*
> *And so I choose this instant as the one to offer to*
> *the Holy*
> *Spirit, that his blessing may descend on us and*
> *keep us in peace.*[2]

I was then reminded of a recent lecture I had given on how apologizing brings the love back. I immediately brought the three of us together and we discussed what had just occurred. Twenty minutes before, we had engaged in one of our worst family fights, but within minutes we experienced healing in our relationship. Healing that began with saying "I'm sorry." I chose love by inviting the Holy Spirit to bring healing into our relationship.

Later, I said to my son, "This will happen in your home. You will have fights with your wife and your children, but what are you going to do afterward? I hope you always remember that the words *I'm sorry* bring the love back."

"I can see that," he said.

Someone else gave me an example of how "I'm sorry" worked in her life. She had an argument with her husband and told me that she wasn't going to apologize because she always has to do it.

"Do you love your husband?" I asked.

"Yes."

"Do you want to stay married to him?"

"Yes."

"Well then *someone* has to do it!"

The following week she called to thank me because she had apologized to her husband and had a wonderful weekend with him.

When conflict breaks out in a relationship, we tend to think that the other person is at fault. Again, someone has to do it. The problem becomes that we want the other person to do it! You may not have started the argument, but if one ensues, you played a part in it. It's not a matter of who's right or wrong. Do you want to heal your relationship or not?

When you don't apologize and at some point communicate about what occurred, resentments build. People have told me about fights with others, and when I ask them if they discussed it they say, "No. It will blow over." It blows over all right, leaving much resentment in its wake.

The lack of honest communication destroys many relationships. The key words here are "honest communication." You don't just apologize to keep the peace. That will not promote mutual healing because you'll still be harboring anger, which decays into resentment. Before you apologize, you must first be by yourself to heal the anger in your heart. Don't do this without asking for Divine assistance.

There have been many times when I've said to the Holy Spirit, "There is no way I can apologize without your help!" It is always there. Once I've resolved my inner turmoil (through prayer, meditation and/or writing) and have come to peace, when I then communicate with my husband, for instance, we are able to honestly talk about how each of us were feeling and why we said the things we did. I honestly believe that my husband and I harbor no resentment toward each other because we communicate after every altercation. Thus we learn more about one another and ourselves. After every fight we've ever had, our relationship has risen to a higher level because we talked about it.

Being less than a perfect human being, my willingness to invite God's Spirit into all of my relationships has brought much healing and peace into my life. When you can own what is yours, when you can apologize whether or not you are right or wrong, you practice love on purpose.

LESSON THREE

Pretend That It Didn't Happen

I read about a minister who played a game with herself. Whenever someone said or wrote something derogatory about her, she would pretend that it didn't happen and treat the person accordingly. This didn't really sink in when I read it, but a few days later someone said something that really ticked me off!

Suddenly, I heard the Inner Voice, 'Sheryl, we are going to pretend that didn't happen.'

'But it did happen! And I didn't like it!' I silently exclaimed.

I heard again, '*Sheryl*, we are going to pretend that didn't happen.'

'All right! Okay! I'm going to pretend that it didn't happen.'

And with those thoughts, I let it go. Remarkably, I was then able to interact with her as if nothing had happened. Through pretending that it didn't happen, I released myself from pain. And just as profoundly, I released her. Think about it: When we hold onto the thoughtless behavior of others, we hurt ourselves and the other person by letting them know, on some level, that they hurt us. By letting it go, we put out a forgiving energy and somehow the other person receives it and reflects it back to us.

In order to practice love, you must think thoughts of love on purpose. I've thought about why sometimes I feel so loving and at other times I feel like a beast. When I'm feeling like a beast it's because I've chosen to think beastly thoughts. By choosing the teacher of love, you come to see that other people behave in a beastly manner for the same reason you do. Hurting people hurt people. When other people hurt you, you cannot heal the relationship by hurting them back. But you also cannot heal a relationship by continuing to let that person hurt you.

The choice for love does not advocate that you become a doormat. If you are in an abusive relationship, do not pretend that abuse is not happening. Inviting the Holy Spirit into the relationship heals your mind. Thus in time, or hopefully right away, you will come to realize that abuse is not love. With your Spirit's help, you can love and forgive him or her and yet still leave the relationship if necessary. Through leaving it in love rather than fear, however, you won't be attracted to similar situations in the future. The cycle is broken.

Love Does Not React

Is there anyone in your life who can bring a certain tone to his or her voice, and upon hearing it you immediately react? One night, my husband came home from work and spoke to me with that "tone" in his voice. In the past I'd react to it and an argument ensued. This time I said, "Honey, if you want to get in a fight, you're going to have to find someone else because I am not in the mood!" He walked out of the room and left by the front door. A moment later, I heard the front door slam and my husband yell, "Honey! I'm home!" He came into the kitchen and started kissing me. Obviously his behavior changed the whole context of the evening.

So here's the lesson: I chose not to react to his tone of voice and in turn, he responded to my not reacting. In any situation you can react in fear or respond with love. My husband's response to my not reacting was a choice for love.

Fear, remember, is on automatic pilot, which means that we automatically react to someone without thinking. But with a desire to practice love on purpose, you will learn to stop before you react and make another choice.

Love Sees the Good

Whenever something bad happens in life, some well-meaning person tells us that something good will come of it. But while immersed in the bad, we might find such rhetoric irritating to say the least. In my 20s, in the midst of what I saw as my life falling apart, a friend said, "Well, at least you've got your health." I felt like shoving her out of the car! I didn't realize it at the time, but she was seeing the good in the situation. I have since discovered that we need not wait for something good to come out of something bad. The good is here now.

A definition of "good" is "free of distress or pain." Interesting. When you focus on what is bad or wrong about a person or circumstance, you do feel distress or pain. The Holy Spirit, however, can use all life experiences to teach you the lessons of love: 'Dear Holy Spirit, help me see the good here.' This simple request can free you of distress and pain.

The good in the universe is omnipresent. But through the lens of fear, we separate from one another and from God, and thus deny the ever present good.

When you allow fear to block your awareness of love, you see a fear-filled world. But the same world, looked at through the eyes of love, is no longer your enemy for you have chosen to be its friend. Asking the Holy Spirit to show you the good in any person or circumstance is practicing love on purpose.

LESSON SIX

Send Thoughts of Love

Once I began to learn about love, I was guided to send love to people. It sounds silly, but it took a few months of practice before I could do it, and years before I could do it consistently. It's not that I didn't want to do it, but I'd forget. Ultimately, I realized that sending thoughts of love was difficult because I had so many blocks in front of my love. As I began to uncover and heal those blocks, I was able to bless others (and myself) with love. I silently send love to people on the freeway (usually after I've yelled, "You

Idiot!"), in the store, or wherever. Sometimes I still feel silly and wonder if it accomplishes anything. But I notice that when I do it, I feel peaceful.

After talking about sending love in a lecture, a participant said that she had tried this and although she did recognize the absence of ego, she didn't "feel" love. I reminded her that love is not just a feeling, love is a choice.

When you silently bless others with love, you are not thinking about the bills that have to be paid, or about who did you wrong yesterday; instead, in that moment you are in harmony with the loving energy of the universe. You are in harmony with God. This is a powerful practice.

LESSON SEVEN

Love Is Your Power

It's not that God is a loving being, God *is* love. Stop. Close your eyes and say, "God is Love." Say it again. And again. Embrace it. Love is energy. Did you feel it? Energy is available power. Electricity is available power. But you will not experience the power of electricity until you flip that switch. Love is available power that you can tap into at any time. Love *is* your power. God = Love = Available Power. But again, love is a choice. When you choose to love, you come home to your power. Not the power to conquer, but the power to heal.

"How Do I Love Myself?"

Have you felt unlovable? Have you felt that if people saw the real you they would recoil in horror? The truth is that the real you *is* love. But this awareness is hidden beneath so much fear. The ego (fear) looks for love in all the wrong places: other people, money, status, and so on. But the Holy Spirit can teach you to look for it where it is, within.

We cannot heal feelings of being unlovable by ourselves. There wouldn't be an inner teacher of love if we didn't need one. And we do need one! I have an aggressive and intense personality. If I could be taught to love myself, trust me on this, the Holy Spirit can help anyone! But again, love is a choice. When you let your Inner Spirit teach you how to love other people on purpose, you will return to the remembrance that you are love.

LESSON NINE

"How Do I Love God?"

When Jesus is asked what the most important commandments are, his reply is to love God with all your heart, mind and soul, and to love your neighbor as yourself.

I pondered this for years. "How do I love God?" Over time, the Holy Spirit taught me that the two commandments are really one and the same. We love God when we love one another. When you practice love on purpose, you come to the profound realization that you and God, God and your neighbor, are not two, but one. There is no separation in love. When you separate from other people, you separate from God's love. You cannot love alone. You cannot heal alone. Love heals you, but it is a collaborative venture.

Love On Purpose

If you feel that you have not been given enough love, decide today to be a giver of love. It sounds simple to decide to be a loving person, but of course, we know that it is not. You don't have to love everyone today. Instead, each day, decide to love one more human being. Hold a door open for someone, smile at another, a "thank you" to someone else. Love need not be complicated.

The ultimate goal of humanity is to love one another. Your consistent willingness to choose love is the pinnacle of spiritual maturity. It's the mountaintop. It's what you are here to learn. You won't learn how to love overnight. You're not supposed to. Learning to love is the task of a lifetime.

God is not looking for perfect people to do his work. If so, let's face it, he'd have a very small work force. God needs every one of us. The love of God can only be extended on this earth through people who become willing to extend it. Take this idea seriously and you will come to know that love truly is—power.

And so, as you go about your life, recognize that the time to love is now. If not you, who? If not now, when? Each day, become willing to ask and heed the question, "How can I love today?" Thus, love begins to permeate and embrace your life. Practice love on purpose as if your *life* depended on it. It does.

PRACTICE FORGIVENESS

Forgiveness has totally changed my life. It will change yours too. Forgiveness is addressed throughout this book because it is the cornerstone of spiritual practice. If you desire healing, forgiveness is not an option—it's a requirement. There is nothing more important than learning how to give and receive love. We cannot love without forgiveness because it's forgiveness that returns to our awareness that we are love. Just as love is something we do on purpose, so is forgiveness.

Love is a choice. Forgiveness is also a choice that cannot be based on emotions. If you don't want to forgive someone because you feel angry and hurt, you will remain angry and hurt until you forgive. It is the very practice of forgiveness that heals your painful emotions. The great news is that you don't need to forgive by yourself, in fact, you can't; but you do need the willingness to forgive. God will take it from there.

Sometimes, however, gathering the willingness to forgive can seem to be as difficult as actually doing it. As one of my friends says, "Dear God, please help me be willing to be willing!" That said, let's explore the practice of forgiveness.

Misconceptions about Forgiveness
No other spiritual principle is more misunderstood than that of forgiveness. Perhaps that's because forgiveness is thought to condone wrong behavior. We can fall into, "I was hurt. I was betrayed.

What he did was wrong, and I just can't forgive him. If I forgive, I am saying that what he did was not wrong."

A woman in her 60s told me that she has not spoken to her mother for years because her mother had been so abusive in her childhood. I mentioned forgiveness. She vehemently replied, "If I forgive her she wins, and I lose!"

"No," I said, "if you *don't* forgive her, she wins and you lose." I later realized that when we harbor unforgiveness—no one wins.

Someone else told me that she didn't think forgiveness worked because, "I've forgiven my husband and he hasn't changed!"

"You don't forgive people so that they will change," I replied. "You forgive them so that you will change."

Forgiveness has nothing to do with another person. The most important understanding about forgiveness is that it is not about them. Forgiveness heals *your* mind. The difficult practice of forgiveness becomes somewhat easier when you recognize that it sets you free from your self-imposed hell.

Forgiveness Is Your Purpose

We are here to learn how to forgive. In fact, *A Course in Miracles* tells us that forgiveness is our function here on earth.[3] Consequently, we will have plenty of opportunities to practice it. It stands to reason that if forgiveness is our purpose, we are going to do things to one another that require forgiveness. Think about it: If no one ever hurts you in any way, how are you going to learn how to forgive?

When it comes to forgiveness, we mostly think about the offenses that others have done to us. But have you ever done anything to someone that he or she might be trying to forgive? We have hurt people and people have hurt us. Perhaps we could begin to view those who have hurt or betrayed us, not as adversaries, not as mother, father, sister, brother—acquaintance, friend or lover, but as spiritual companions. We are all in this together so that we might teach one another the most important lessons one could ever learn, to let it go, to forgive. With this understanding you then become grateful for all who touch your life, even those who treat you in a harmful way. He or she gives you yet another opportunity to understand and to experience the healing power of forgiveness.

Forgive Yourself

We can only give what we are willing to receive. The practice of forgiveness begins with us. We must forgive ourselves because on a level we are probably not conscious of, we may feel that if we were worth loving, other people would have loved us more; if we were worth loving, other people would not have hurt us. Ask the Spirit Within to help you forgive yourself for forgetting that you are worthy of love.

Forgiveness starts with your willingness to be free of emotional pain. It is a deep inner work that occurs throughout your life. You may have said or done something unkind to another person. Or you may feel guilt over a past relationship that ended because of divorce, death or some other way. And of course, we have a multitude of experiences that we may feel bad or sad about.

Without the willingness to forgive yourself, you will continue to perpetuate pain in your interaction with other people. Although self-forgiveness is an ongoing process, begin by recognizing that there is a Presence within you that can heal you. God is truly the love with which you can forgive yourself. Meditate and reflect on this until the reality of it begins to permeate your mind and heart. As it begins to dawn on you that you are loved and forgiven, you will automatically extend that to other people. Life gets better.

Take Another Look At Your Childhood

We are all familiar with the term "dysfunctional childhood." This has become an over used and often misunderstood concept. I think of a dysfunctional family as any family with more than one person in it! A dysfunctional childhood does not necessarily mean that your parents, siblings, teachers or anyone else abused you.

In order to gain better understanding let's pick apart the word "dysfunctional." The word "functional" means "capable of serving the purpose for which it was designed." "Dys" is a combining form that means; "ill; bad; impaired processes." We were created from the Source of Love. We were designed to serve the purpose of extending that love. Somewhere along the way we forgot this important truth and so in a sense, our knowledge of our purpose became impaired. In this context, "dysfunctional childhood" simply means that we grew up surrounded by people who were impaired in their ability to come forth with unconditional love.

It is important to understand that your parents or whoever hurt you were also products of their dysfunctional past. If you were to research your parent's childhood, you just might fall to your knees and thank God that they did a better job than their parents. With the awareness that everyone we have met also had a dysfunctional past, forgiveness becomes an easier process because it facilitates the understanding that when we are in emotional pain, we all too often inflict our pain onto others.

Healing cannot enter a relationship from the level of "You really hurt me, but I am going to forgive you." Healing comes through prayer for your own healing: 'Dear God, I *am* hurt. Please teach me how to forgive.' Such a prayer facilitates the awareness that forgiveness must start with you. The willingness to forgive anyone whom you feel has wronged you will set you free. Forgiveness does not condone negative behavior, but it does set you free of the anger, pain and hatred within your own heart. Forgiveness breaks the cycle of hurt people hurting people.

"But Do We Have To Go To Lunch?"
You may not want to forgive certain people, however, because you don't want to see them again. This is not a good reason to remain unforgiving because forgiveness heals you. Through your own healing, you may want to reconcile with another person or you may not.

To reconcile is to bring to harmony. But this does not mean that you have to set up a lunch date. Some say that if you don't want to see someone, you have not really forgiven him or her. Not so. Many people have sought and found peace through forgiving someone who has died. This can occur because forgiveness is not about another person; it's not about changing the past, rather, it's about healing our perceptions of the past. Such healing is an inside job and does not require the presence of another person. It requires willingness and God.

Throughout our lives we have relationships with many people, and those encounters offer us numerous opportunities to practice forgiveness and experience healing. We have all had friendships that have faded away, issues with co-workers and numerous casual encounters that have left us with feelings of anger, pain or betrayal. Whether or not we interact with them again, negative feelings toward anyone must be forgiven if we want to live purposeful and happy lives.

When you work with forgiveness and come to peace about someone, then healing has been accomplished. If you refuse to see people without first forgiving them, you remain imprisoned. If you are thinking that you don't want to forgive someone because you want him out of your life, make another choice. Haven't you noticed that the people you don't forgive are always lurking in your mind? If you really want someone out of your life—forgive!

On the other hand, some relationships require not only forgiveness, but also reconciliation. I went through a major forgiveness challenge with a family member where I thought, 'Okay, I'll forgive her, but I never want to see her again!' I knew that was not the right decision because it did not facilitate peace. If you are not at peace about someone, you are not done with forgiveness whether or not you see him or her again. Don't kid yourself. Also, don't beat up on yourself—forgiveness is hard work.

Layers of Healing

Forgiveness is a process and a practice. You may have forgiven someone and feel at peace about him or her. A few years later, however, you realize that there is more healing work to be done. Healing is a process because we are not emotionally or spiritually prepared to deal with our wounds all at once. This is why something that happened in childhood can erupt into your life at age thirty, forty, fifty or beyond. It comes to the surface when you are emotionally and spiritually ready to deal with it. If you attempted to look at and deal with your emotional wounds all at once, you'd probably have a nervous breakdown!

Spiritual healing can be likened to eating an artichoke: Peeling off one layer at a time, finally coming to the core—the heart. We have layer upon layer of fear covering our heart, but with forgiveness we shed these layers one at a time and return to love.

Forgive and Forget

"Well I'll forgive her, but I won't forget!" We have all heard that and may have been there. Forgiving and not forgetting is not forgiveness, but denial. If we continue to view a person only through his or her past mistakes, we overlook the healing that can occur in the present. To forgive and forget, however, doesn't mean that you suddenly get amnesia. Let's say that you have gone through a divorce. With much inner work you have come to forgiveness and consequently, you are at peace with your ex. This doesn't mean that you will no longer remember what occurred in the relationship; but it will be forgotten in the sense that you no longer feel pain around it, and have no desire to hold anything against the other person.

To forget is to fail to mention. When we have been hurt, betrayed or rejected, talking and thinking about it all the time will not facilitate the willingness to forgive and forget. And sure, it's totally normal to think and talk about it, that's part of the healing process, but for how long? If you're still thinking and talking about what someone did to you in 1973, it's time to forgive!

Frankly, after years of practicing forgiveness, I have come to the point where if the incident occurred longer than two hours ago it's time to forgive. As you realize that forgiveness frees you, you will quickly want to get on with it.

Forgiveness Alleviates Fear

To my amazement, a byproduct of the consistent practice of forgiveness is that I no longer live in fear of death, taxes and terrorists. When our minds are filled with unforgiveness (resentment, hatred, fear and guilt) this world looks like a dangerous and scary place. Fear separates us from one another, God and our true Self.

We have been told that perfect love casts out fear. Having been created by perfect Love, we can never be separated from it. Having also been created in the image of God when we forgive, we reflect God's love here on earth. This is our purpose. As we fulfill this purpose, we see that we are in union with every living thing— we see a world where fear has been replaced by Love.

Forgiveness Calls Forth Your Gifts

Acts of betrayal and rejection have left us with emotional wounds, but God can reach us through those wounds. When pain becomes intolerable we are more likely to allow God's presence into our mind and heart. As you transcend pain through the practice of forgiveness, you will find that you have gifts and talents you never knew you had. Forgiveness facilitates the emergence of your gifts into the world. I had never planned to teach spirituality, but once I began to heal my emotional wounds through forgiveness my gifts in this area seemed to erupt from me.

Prior to my spiritual work I was pent-up with anger and frustration. As I began to practice forgiveness, my spirit burst forth with something to say. It was almost as if I didn't have a choice in the matter. This may occur in your life too.

So now that we've delved into the importance of forgiveness, how do we go about doing it?

Forgive The Past

Forgiveness requires a willingness to let go of the past. Don't forget that the past was not only your childhood, but also this morning. In order to heal, you must become willing to look at your past without staying stuck in it. The problem for many of us is that we have not only looked at our past—we've pitched a tent there!

Make a list of the people or events that, in your perception, caused you to feel rejected, humiliated, unworthy, guilty or unlovable. In each case, write down what happened. Allow yourself to feel it all. This is important because if you are feeling pain in some area of your life right now, it probably stems from the people or events on that list. We continually shadow the pain from the past onto the present.

This forgiveness exercise will enable you to look at your past and ultimately let it go. Will it be painful to do this work? You bet. But would you rather experience the sharp pain that precipitates healing, or continue living with a dull ache for the rest of your life?

As you move through the people on your list, you may find it helpful to work with this effectual prayer:

> *I give you to the Holy Spirit as part of myself.*
> *I know that you will be released,*
> *unless I want to use you to imprison myself.*
> *In the name of my freedom*
> *I choose your release,*
> *because I recognize that we will be*
> *released together.*[4]

You exist in a prison of your own making. When you condemn others you are chained to them, jailing them and imprisoning yourself. Forgiveness frees you from the vacillating roles of jailer and prisoner. As you begin to recognize the value of forgiveness, you will no longer want to use the actions of other people to hurt yourself.

Every Day Forgiveness

Forgiveness is not something you do once and then experience a healed life. It is a process and a practice. Life gives us opportunities to practice forgiveness every single day. In thought, project yourself to tomorrow morning. It's 9 a.m. Someone just said something that really made you angry. By 10:30 you have already yelled at one of your co-workers, spilled coffee all over your desk, and told off a client. At 5:15 you're on the freeway—screaming at everyone! At 6:00 you arrive home, yell at your kids, kick your dog and spit at your husband.

Let's try it again. It's 9 a.m. Someone just said something that really upset you. But this time you remember, 'Hmmm, I read that chapter on forgiveness last night, maybe I'll try it. What have I got to lose?' Even though you may have ongoing issues with the person, just for a moment be willing to forgive. Be willing to see the situation from a higher, more loving perception: 'Dear God, I am willing to forgive _____. Please help me see him with your loving vision.' Now it's 10:30. You have not yelled at anyone, and you may have caught that coffee cup before it spilled.

Our minds are filled with grievances, which is why we must practice forgiveness every single day. Every day? Absolutely. Think about it; the person who cuts you off on the freeway, or the one who makes an unkind remark, or the co-worker who irritates you—all provide opportunities to practice forgiveness. With this kind of spiritual practice you begin to live in the present, transform your day, and thus your life.

Three Steps to Forgiveness

Forgiveness must be learned from the same Inner Presence that teaches us how to love. The first step in the process is awareness that you are harboring negative thoughts toward other people, and that these negative thoughts are only hurting you. The second step is the willingness to be released from your pain: 'Dear God, I don't know how to forgive. I don't even know if I want to, but I do know that I am willing to be free of pain. Please help me.' The third step belongs to God. Your part is to ask God to do for you what you cannot do for yourself.

The Practice

This three-step process sounds easy, but we all know that it is not. The first two steps are our part in the process and that's where the inner work comes in. I have been practicing forgiveness for many years and could probably write an entire book on just my own experiences. At this point I can get down to forgiveness fairly quickly because I know that it will facilitate peace. This doesn't mean that it's easy—only easier in that I really want peace and I will forgive anyone to have it.

When I am angry and hurt I start with prayer, usually the one I shared earlier in this chapter. I also frequently use a guided meditation on forgiveness that I have found incredibly helpful over the years.[5] Writing is another way to get it off your chest, to let it out. In your willingness to let it out, you make room to let God's love in.

Recently I had a forgiveness challenge. One where I was so angry that I didn't want to forgive, and was even irked that I had to! As I drove home that day, I was totally enraged and actually felt the rage wrapping around my heart (the real cause of heart attacks, in my opinion). I knew that although I didn't want to forgive, I had to. I came home and prayed, I did a long meditation on forgiveness, I begged God to help me do what I did not (but obviously did) want to do. Within twelve hours my anger was suddenly gone and I was able to call the person with love in my heart not pain.

This has happened so many times in my relationships. I'm angry; I feel that I cannot forgive. I pray, I meditate and then invariably through no strength of my own, I am able to allow God's forgiveness to flow through me.

On an every-day basis when I catch myself thinking negatively about a person, I release it as soon as possible by thinking: 'God is the love in which I forgive you; God is the love in which I forgive myself.' Or, 'I forgive and release you; I bless you with God's love.' The words don't really matter. The important thing is that instead of continuing to negatively spin on the person, make a higher choice. Invite God's love into your mind and heart. Sometimes this practice alone can release grievances and negativity in a few minutes, other times it takes more inner work. In any case, desire to let it go will work. Your very willingness to pray allows God to work in and through you.

Forgive Through Me

In *The Hiding Place*, Corrie ten Boom gives us a wonderful example of how God forgives through us. She was a Christian woman who hid Jews in her attic during the Holocaust. She was eventually caught and sent to prison. After her release, she later gave talks about her prison experiences.

One night, she was at a church service in Munich and saw a man who had been one of her jailers while in prison. The man came up to her and told her that he was grateful for her message of forgiveness. "His hand was thrust out to shake mine. And I, who had preached so often on the need to forgive, kept my hand at my side."

Angry, vengeful thoughts boiled through her. She tried to smile. She struggled to raise her hand to shake his. She could not. She said a silent prayer, "God, I cannot forgive him. Give me your forgiveness." Then, as she shook his hand the most incredible thing happened. A current seemed to pass from her to him, and into her heart sprang a love for this stranger that almost overwhelmed her.

She discovered that it is not *our* forgiveness that heals the world, but God's forgiveness flowing through us.

Love Your Enemies

This means, forgive your enemies. We long to experience God's grace, love and forgiveness, yet we can only experience this as we allow God to extend through us to other people. When we are told to love our enemies along with that command, at the very asking, we are given Love itself.

Do You Need to Forgive God?

Some people are mad at God because this or that happened, forgetting that "this" or "that" happens to everyone. If we live long enough each one of us will have had multiple experiences of hurt, betrayal and rejection. We will have experienced loss, grief and emotional pain. God is not the cause of your pain. God is the only presence that can heal your pain. If you leave God out of the loop, make God into the big scapegoat in the sky, where do you go for healing? You cannot heal yourself by yourself.

As you allow God's light to shine on your sorrows you begin to truly live. You find new purpose and meaning in the realization that you are not the only one who has suffered. All have suffered. Then, in your own way, you become an instrument for God's use that brings healing not only to yourself, but also to your relationships. If you are mad at God, it's time to get over it.

You Are Needed

God needs you—your hands, your feet, your voice, and your will—to extend love and forgiveness into the world. Many people don't believe in God, but some of those same people believe in you. Will you speak God's words? Will you allow God's love and forgiveness to flow through you?

We may think that we don't contribute to the negativity in the world, but we do. Every time we turn our back on another, judge or condemn, we contribute to the negative energy in this world, even when it's done in God's name. God is not a god of condemnation, but God *is* Love.

As you go about your life, you need not ask God to forgive you, for that Presence has never condemned you. Ask instead that you may learn how to forgive. Therein lies your freedom, and peace.

DEALING WITH PEOPLE
WHO DRIVE YOU NUTS!

Dear God, grant me the serenity to accept the things
I cannot change, the courage to change the things I can,
and the wisdom to hide the bodies of all the people I had
to kill because they drove me nuts![6]

The people who make us crazy are those who don't do what we want them to do. Unconsciously, we assign roles to people. Perhaps we assign our significant other the role of being constantly loving and supportive. We may assign our children the role of being ideal representations of us. Our friends, co-workers and of course, our parents, are often assigned the impossible role of perfection; as well as being assigned the equally impossible role of appreciating our perfection.

When you are angry at someone, isn't it because he or she failed to live up to the role you allotted them? Of course killing them is not the answer. Giving up your role for them is. Healing relationships demands that you be willing to take a deeper look at yourself.

Jean-Paul Sartre said, "Hell, is other people." But really, hell is our *reactions* to other people. No one is going to change until you do, and while disturbing, it's true.

An acquaintance said, "I don't like coming to your lectures because they are always about me! How come there is never anything wrong with the other person?" We laughed. She was going through a difficult divorce at the time, so I could see her point.

Taking a look at yourself doesn't mean that "they" aren't doing anything. You are not responsible for another person's behavior, but you are responsible for *your* reactions to their behavior.

We react to other people based not on reality, but on our perception of reality. Most of the time, people who upset us are simply marching to the beat of their own drum, yet we perceive their behavior as being specifically designed to make us nuts. The people with whom we have conflict are not punishments sent from the universe; rather, we have attracted one another so that we might teach and learn the lessons of love and forgiveness.

A big part of spiritual practice is letting go of your expectations of what others should be for you, and instead asking the Spirit Within for a higher interpretation. As you allow the Inner Presence to return your mind to love, that love will be reflected in your relationships.

Do You Want To Be Happy Or Right?

A concept from *A Course in Miracles* that has precipitated much healing in my life comes to light in the very poignant question: *Do you want to be happy or right?*[7] Those words jumped out at me because I was the Queen of Being Right. I thought, 'Dear God, I am willing to give up a lot of stuff, but please don't make me give up being right!' It was, and continues to be my greatest challenge.

Isn't being right a very satisfying experience? When I first became aware of this concept, someone sent me an inflammatory letter. On my morning walk as I mentally prepared a defense, I heard, 'Sheryl, do you want to be happy or do you want to be right?'

'But dear God, in this situation being right would make me *extremely* happy!'

This discourse went on because in that situation "right" and "happy" seemed like the same thing. As I heard the higher part of my mind whisper, 'Sheryl, choose again,' I had to laugh at myself.

So I did not respond to the letter to defend my position. I refused to add fuel to the fire just because I was right. Instead, I chose happiness when I let it go.

Choosing happiness over being right is one of the hardest principles to practice because your ego will exclaim, 'What! You're just going to let her get away with that? You're going to let him think that about you?' The truth is, "they" are going to think "that" about you anyway, especially if you throw your stuff at them. My problem is I usually am right (and humble too!). Nevertheless, I have learned time and time again that when I have to make someone else wrong so that I can be right, I'm not happy. I want to be happy. And you?

"Oh My God. It's ME!"

I had so many conflicts at one point in my life that I finally had to recognize the common denominator in every conflict situation— Me! Many years ago, I had an experience I will never forget. While running errands, I went to four places in approximately twenty minutes, and met up with four angry people! After four conflicts in such a short time, I got into my car and said aloud, "Sheryl, I don't know *what* you are doing and I don't know *how* you are doing it, but somehow you *are* doing this!" Four conflicts in twenty minutes brought me to a rude awakening: Oh My God. It's Me!

This recognition is life changing, and when reached, you invite the universe to help you. Prior to my four-in-twenty experience, I had already formed a practice of listening to inspirational recordings every day. Once I realized that the anger was in me, it seemed that every recording I listened to was about anger. Maybe I had been guided to teachings on anger all along, but I didn't hear that part. I could not apply the teachings to myself until I realized that I was the problem. As long as I thought that my anger was caused by what other people were doing to me, I was unable to receive guidance on healing it.

Once I began meditating every day, the first change I noticed was that I no longer had as many angry and conflict filled situations. Why? In meditation I contacted a place of inner peace, and then peace instead of anger began to extend through me.

> **Awareness Exercise**
> *Make a list of the people who drive you nuts. And ask, 'What is it about that person that upsets me so much? What is being triggered in me?' You can also reflect on, 'When in my life and with whom, have I felt the same way? Did I feel invalidated by my parents, teachers, bosses, or my religion? Did I feel abandoned or rejected by someone in the past? When, where, and with whom have I felt this before?' There was always another time. You have taken that other time and shadowed it onto those in your present relationships. When you recognize this and take full responsibility for it, you begin to heal your present relationships through forgiving the past. (Review chapter "Practice Forgiveness.")*

Healing In Family Relationships

I read a card that said, "There are those who love you because of who you are; there are those who love you because of who you appear to be. And then there's your family: Those who love you because they have to—it's like a law or something!"

Family relationships have the potential to challenge our spiritual maturity more than any other relationship. Our family is part of who we are. Nevertheless, we can walk into a family gathering feeling like an alien. Why is it that we can meditate every day, work on ourselves ad nauseam and then walk into a family gathering and revert to age 16! We often don't even realize that this is happening. Within the family dynamic we don't really see each other as we truly are, we see each other through the lens of our unhealed past.

Stop thinking of your family as people that screwed you up, and instead think of them as people that served to guide you to your destiny. Without what went on in your family, you would not be who you are. When you begin to deal with your family (including in-laws) from a level of love and forgiveness, only then can you more fully be who you are meant to be.

A friend told me that in the process of forgiving her mother she focused on all the wonderful things her mother had done for her instead of focusing on the mistakes she had made. When she shared this insight with her mother, it facilitated healing in their relationship.

Family gatherings offer many opportunities for spiritual practice. You can experience much joy and healing in this class-room when you learn to prepare in advance. You can prepare in advance by working with forgiveness toward the people whom you already know will push your buttons.

One year before Thanksgiving I thought about someone I would have to visit who triggered tension within me. So I decided to prepare in advance. For two weeks, on my morning walk I took along a mediation tape on forgiveness and practiced forgiving her. I said to a friend, "I'm going to have to do this every day between now and November 27th—mind you, it's only the 11th!" She laughed and replied, "Well at least you work at it."

My work didn't end there however. On the way to the event, I surrendered the situation to God and asked that my heart be opened to give and receive love. But ten minutes from the house, I began to think about everything she had done that upset me. And then I heard the Inner Voice, 'Sheryl, that all happened in the past. She can be seen anew in this moment.' I heard it and thought, 'That's true.' I got it! I had experienced a tense, difficult relationship with her for over five years. But in that moment, I saw her anew. I no longer feel tension in her presence. So what changed? I changed. Instead of letting my ego take charge, I chose the Higher Presence to help heal my relationship.

It never ceases to amaze me that when I change—other people change! I wonder, 'Was I the only jerk in this relationship?' The truth is that through your own healing work, you begin to put out a different energy and other people respond in kind.

Healing On the Job

In my office many people talk to me about their work. I have noticed that relationships in the workplace are similar to family relationships. We are usually unconscious of this dynamic, but it is something I have observed time and time again. In the workplace, we might project the role of parent onto our boss, while our co-workers become our siblings. If you felt that your siblings always got more than you did, or that Dad loved your brother best, you might project these feelings onto your boss and your co-workers. Obviously, not everyone does this, and even if one does it is mostly unconscious. Calling attention to the dynamics in family relationships and noticing if they are similar to work relationships could provide a profound avenue for healing in both areas. Be willing to give this some thought.

In any case, most people with a job often encounter someone who drives them nuts. Work relationships can trigger unconscious stuff within us because in our daily life, we choose to surround ourselves with people who are like us, those of like mind, however dysfunctional that may be. But the work environment offers opportunities to interact with different personalities and opinions; people who are not necessarily like us; people who we might not choose to interact with. You've probably noticed that this occurs in family relationships as well.

You may not have control over what other people are doing, but you do have control over how you respond to them. If someone's behavior upsets you, what do you do? Do you stew about it all day long—for weeks or even *years*? A higher choice is made when you recognize that you need not be affected by another person's negative behavior. You need not let another person rule your state of mind.

I had a receptionist who complained that the UPS man was rude and unfriendly. "Okay," I replied, "let's do an experiment. Every day, silently send him love and see what happens." A few days later she said, "I can't believe it! He's totally changed!" Who really changed? She did. When we change the content of the energy that we are putting forth, other people appear to change as well.

Sometimes our work environments can seem like a loveless place, but the infusion of our love and forgiveness can change it. Spiritual practice is this: You get to work and by 9:15 you've forgotten all about love and forgiveness and, 'Darn it, if that person says one more thing to me …!' But then, at 12:15 you remember, 'Oh yeah, I read that chapter last night, something about love and forgiveness … okay, I forgive her, I release her, I bless her with love.' You will have a new kind of day.

Healing In Abusive Relationships

In our civilized society we are encouraged to stop physical abuse; however, verbal abuse is much more prevalent and is a major crime of the spirit. Over the years, many people have told me about such abuse in their workplace, and I wonder why they put up with it. If you are in such an environment, recognize that you were attracted to it for a reason. The lesson and subsequent growth comes through standing up for yourself. People who stand up for themselves are rarely fired. If you are fired after doing so, I suggest that you thank God!

A patient told me that her boss screamed at everyone in the office on a daily basis. She finally couldn't stand it anymore and quit. A few days later her boss called and offered her the job back, with a raise. She told him she would not work for him if he continued his abusive behavior. He promised that he would never do it again. "Has he?" I asked. "No." "Does he yell at everyone else in the office?" I asked. "Yes," she replied, "he screams at everyone but me." Her boss no longer treats her that way because she no longer allows it.

Understand a profound truth: In any relationship, people treat you the way you allow them to. You must come to a place of honoring yourself so that you no longer tolerate or allow abusive behavior of any kind. Once you do that, you are not only helping yourself, but the abuser as well. The person who is abusing you yearns for healing just as you do. He or she may accept the lesson, the healing, or not. But you will have gained healing by honoring yourself.

Prepare In Advance

Previously, I spoke about this idea in regard to family relationships, but it obviously applies to all relationships. Most of us interact with at least one person who, in our perception causes us pain. Perhaps it is a family member, a co-worker or an ex-spouse. You may not have realized this but before you see him or her, you probably do prepare in advance. You prepare to be hopping mad!

Instead of preparing to be angry, make another choice. Those people that upset you over and over again can be your greatest teachers. In fact, you owe them gratitude because they show you, *you*! These people can be stumbling blocks on your spiritual path or stepping-stones to your spiritual growth. What choice will you make?

Call to mind a person with whom you are experiencing

conflict, and bring awareness to what he or she does that bothers you. Next, pay attention to how you react to what has been done. Do you get angry? Defensive? Resentful? Constricted? Tense? The two of you have set up a dynamic. He or she does something and then you react. You generally know when you will see these people, so prepare in advance to make another choice.

Preparation can involve ongoing forgiveness work, but you can also ask for Divine assistance before an interaction. Enter into a space of silence within your mind and ask the Higher Presence to show you a different perception of the person or situation. This simple request can change your reactions and promote real healing in the relationship.

When you begin to change your reactions to the behavior of other people by calling on a higher perception, your relationships will change. They have to, because when you respond differently, it follows that he or she must respond differently too.

Lessons Learned From My Teenager
When I realized that my teenager was getting some kind of payoff from my overt reactions to his negative behavior, I stopped reacting negatively. Lo and behold, he stopped the behavior. We were well into his teens before I figured this out, and of course, opportunities to practice it came up time and time again. In fact, as I write this they are still coming up!

The teen years are especially challenging not only for the parent, but for the teenager as well. Therefore, the opportunities to learn lessons from one another are legion. When my son was thirteen, we got into an argument about something and I took it to the ozone! Afterward as I prayed about it, I kept hearing that I needed to ask for his forgiveness because I was wrong. Do you have any idea how hard it is to tell your thirteen-year-old that you were wrong? My ego screamed, 'I don't think so!' At the time, that was up there with the harder things I had done. I did follow through, however, and it brought much peace between us.

Overall, parenting has served to teach me many spiritual lessons. In fact, I view parenting as a major spiritual path. I've heard that our children are like little Zen masters designed just for us. It's so true. Being a parent has taught me, among many other things that you cannot always judge a person based on his or her behavior. You know the truth of this if you have kids. If we loved our children based only on their behavior—would we love them at all? No way! I have a teenager! No way! Yet somehow, we look beyond their behavior and love them still.

Our behavior does not always reflect who we truly are. Let's face it, we all have bad days. While it is true that aligning our thoughts with love will reflect in our behavior, we still have days when choosing love is difficult. So knowing this, why not give other people a break instead of berating them. Focus instead on your response to their behavior.

Swim By the Hook
A friend gave me this wonderful nugget: Swim by the hook. She raised four sons, and one in particular always tried to engage her and his father in battle. In the midst of these battles, she whispered to her husband, "Honey, swim by the hook." Our children try to hook us into battle. The secret is not to bite.

Swim by the hook is great spiritual wisdom. It's about choosing your battles wisely. When you are in the midst of a battle with another person your view is from the ego's vision, one of fear. When ensconced in the conflict, you must become willing to swim by the hook—to rise above the battleground. You can do this in prayer: 'Dear God, the temptation to attack another has darkened my mind. May you lift me up to a higher place so that, together, we may look upon the battleground and see that it is not

real. Only love is real. Only you O God are real. Return me to your
loving vision. Thank you.'

Save Your Anger for the Next Day

One day, after using the aforementioned prayer, I received the
guidance to save my anger for the next day. Try this some time. It's
not that you deny or repress your anger, but decide instead to save
it for the next day. In the intervening time period, take your anger
into prayer or meditation and ask for a new perception of the situation. Ask for healing to take place within you. Taking these steps
could change your life.

And speaking of meditation … Have you noticed that when
you mediate your grievances and judgments toward other people
often come up? I usually attempt to set those thoughts aside. One
time, however, I was really angry at someone and as my anger
toward her came forth, I let myself flow with it. I let myself feel it.
I then asked God to let me see her from a higher perception.
Suddenly, I felt an amazing love for her. I felt as if an incredible
healing had taken place between us. Did she get it? I don't know.
But I got it. Afterward, I was able to release my grievances toward
her.

The truth is that when you criticize or condemn others, you
attack yourself. When you choose, in an instant, to step back and
see them as they truly are, a spiritual reflection of you, then you
have extended love. God cannot be found alone. God is found in
our interactions with others. But that Presence is only found in
love and forgiveness, not in condemnation and judgment.

Ancient Spiritual Lessons

Regardless of your religion or spiritual beliefs it must be acknowledged that Jesus was a great spiritual teacher especially when it
comes to dealing with people who upset you. It is Jesus who asks,

"Why do you see that splinter in your neighbor's eye, yet fail to see the log in your own?"[8] We look at the faults in others failing to see that we are looking at them through our own distorted vision. We criticize people, point out their failures and lament about their faults, all the while forgetting that we see them through the lens of our own faults and weaknesses.

"Love your enemies and bless those who curse you." You are not asked to be holier-than-thou, rather, you are asked to choose the highest thought, the most loving thought because it releases you. It is not about them, it's about you.

"Eye for eye, tooth for tooth. Is that going to get us anywhere? Here is what I propose: Don't hit back at all. Spiritual maturity does not demand that we never get angry, but rather that we become aware of our anger and take responsibility for those feelings as they come up. Angry thoughts can result in harmful actions. Fortunately, there is another way.

The Way of Love

If you were able to view unloving behavior, even your own, as a dysfunctional way of calling for love, you might come to understand that the appropriate response is to give love. Most of us are not too good at distinguishing between love and a call for love; however, there is a Presence within us that can.

A mediator is an objective person who listens carefully to both parties, then helps them come to a resolution. Your Inner Spirit is a mediator that is always available. When immersed in conflict turn within and commune with that Presence. Be willing to take all of your grievances and judgments, all of them (toward yourself, another gender, race, religion, or political party), and ask for the miracle of a higher vision, a more loving perception. Giving and receiving are the same. When we give judgment and attack, we receive it. When we give love, kindness and understanding, we receive it. Recognize that each person you meet offers an opportunity to give. What do you want to receive?

And so as you go about your life, may you reflect on the following:

> *People cross our lives,*
> *touch it with love, and move on.*
> *There are those who leave us,*
> *and we breathe a sigh of relief*
> *wondering why we came in*
> *contact with them.*
> *And then, there are those who*
> *leave us, and we breathe a sigh of remorse*
> *wondering why they had to go and leave*
> *such a gaping hole.*
> *Children leave parents.*
> *Friends leave friends.*
> *Acquaintances move on.*
> *Lovers grow together or grow apart.*
>
> *I believe in the universal plan for our lives.*
> *God moves people in and out,*
> *each leaving their mark on the other.*
> *As time goes on, we find*
> *that we are made up of bits and pieces*
> *of all who have touched our lives.*
> *We would be less if they had not*
> *touched us,*
> *we are more because they did.*[9]

2 POWER IN A NEW PERCEPTION

Seek not to change the world.
Instead, choose to change
your mind about the world.

– A Course in Miracles

The real voyage of discovery
consists not in seeking new
landscapes, but in having new
eyes.

– Marcel Proust

CHOOSE ANOTHER STREET

L ife is all about choice. Regardless of your circumstances, you always have a choice in how to perceive them. Consider the following:

Autobiography in Five Short Chapters

Chapter One

I walk down the street.

There is a deep hole in the sidewalk.

I fall in.

I am lost … I am helpless.

It isn't my fault.

It takes forever to find a way out.

Chapter Two

I walk down the same street.

There is a deep hole in the sidewalk.

I pretend I don't see it.

I fall in again.

I can't believe I am in this same place.

But, it isn't my fault.

It still takes a long time to get out.

Chapter Three

I walk down the same street.

There is a deep hole in the sidewalk.

I *see* it is there.

I still fall in … it's a habit … but,

my eyes are open.

I know where I am.

It is my fault.

I get out immediately.

Chapter Four

I walk down the same street.

There is a deep hole in the sidewalk

I walk around it.

Chapter Five

I walk down another street. [10]

I first read this autobiography around twenty years ago. I held onto it because even then, I found it brilliant in that it chronicles the emotional and spiritual stages we must go through in order to break out of self-imposed prisons to be free.

Chapter One reveals our tendency to feel victimized, while Chapter Two calls our attention to how we engage in denial. Chapter Three introduces the idea that as we open our eyes to our repetitive thought patterns, we can then take responsibility for them and move on to Chapter Four—personal empowerment. Chapter Five represents freedom through making another choice.

The Victim Mentality

So let's delve into Chapter One. *There is a hole in the sidewalk. I fall in. I am lost. I am helpless. It isn't my fault.* This seems to suggest that there is no other choice: 'The hole is there, what else could I do but fall in?'

In thinking that we are victimized by something outside of us (the hole in this example), we feel lost and helpless. We then look around to find who we can blame for putting the hole there in the first place! Our feelings of victimization are not caused by the hole or by another person, but instead are caused by our thoughts, perceptions and attitudes.

Whenever we think that someone or something is keeping us from moving forward, we play the victim. With such a mentality we feel powerless to change our lives because in *our* perception, the cause of our distress is "out there." We don't see a loving and benevolent universe, but one that is unfair. When we recognize the cause of emotional pain as stemming from our own thoughts, we step forward to change and real growth.

Denial and Projection

In Chapter Two, you walk down the street and the hole is there, but you pretend not to see it ... OOPS! Only to fall in again! Chapter Two is about denial. *I pretend I don't see it. I fall in again.* Denial is a defense mechanism we have devised to deny truth.

A defense mechanism is an unconscious process that protects us from unacceptable or painful ideas. Our defense mechanisms are usually formed in childhood as a protective device. They help us deal with people and events we were not mature enough to deal with at the time.

Someone told me that that she was once in a therapy group discussing something that had happened between her and her mother when she was eight years old. The therapist told her that she had been in denial. She vehemently replied, "How could I have been in denial, I was eight years old!" "Okay, I can see that you have a problem with the word denial," the therapist replied, "so call it George. George was there to protect you when you couldn't do it yourself." Don't you love that? Denial—Call it George!

As adults, denial plays out in such a way that it allows us to avoid seeing what we don't want to see not only in ourselves, but also in other people. In my office I frequently ask patients if they are experiencing stress. By their response, you would think that I had asked them if they killed their mothers! Refusal to acknowledge their stress helps them deny that they have anything to be stressed about. If you are not aware of what is going on in your life, how can you deal with it?

I've heard it said that the truth will set you free, but first, it will make you really mad! Not only do we use denial to avoid the truth, we also use its twin—projection. With projection, we see our unconscious feelings, thoughts and attitudes embodied in another person, place or thing.

Think of projection this way: When you watch a movie, the image on the screen is merely a projection from a movie projector. Your life is your movie, projected from *your* mind. In your movie, you see what you believe you are going to see rather than what is actually there. If you believe that life is a struggle, you project that it is. If you believe that people are up to no good, you project that this is so. If you believe that the world is evil and constantly victimizing you, you will focus on evil and be attracted to or cause situations where you feel victimized—not realizing that you are victimized by your projections.

On the other hand, if you believe that you live in a benevolent universe, one where all things work together for good, you will see the evidence of this in your life. You see what you believe is there. You are the projector of your movie. What is the movie of your life showing you about you?

During the first half of our lives most of us were stuck in chapters One and Two: Feeling like a victim, blaming others and engaging in denial. We fell into the hole again and again, but it was always someone else's fault. Sadly, there are many who live the second half of their lives stuck in chapters One and Two: *I am help-less. It isn't my fault.* If you feel like a victim because of your race, your gender, your sexuality or your past, such thoughts keep you imprisoned. There are people of every race, religion, gender and varied difficult experiences who are living empowering and purposeful lives. They are the people who went on to Chapter Three.

Awareness and Responsibility

In Chapter Three, you fall in the hole, *again*. You realize that you are about to do it, but yet you still do it. Falling in the hole has become a habit. Once you recognize your patterns, however, you come into self-awareness and responsibility: 'My eyes are open, I know where I am. It's me.'

The problem we might have with taking personal responsibility is that, while growing up we may have heard our parents or someone else yell, "Who's responsible for this?"

"Fido!"

We knew that if we admitted being at fault, we would be punished. But in the spiritual realm, awareness and responsibility facilitate healing. How can you heal a negative pattern that you won't own? Owning your "stuff" is not about blaming or beating up on yourself. Blaming yourself will keep you just as stuck as blaming someone or something else. However, until you come to the awareness that cries out "Oh My God. It's Me!" the universe has nothing to work with. God can only work with you on the causal level, which is thought. If God were to just fix your negative patterns, you would fall into the hole again because it is your thoughts that are the problem. The universe does not violate your free will. Once you can say, "It's Me!" you have essentially said to God, 'Come into my mind and shine light on my thoughts. Show me another way.' Even then, you may fall into that hole again and again, but you will gain in awareness and growth.

The level on which we choose our circumstances is incomprehensible to us as human beings. Nevertheless, come to trust that there is a benevolent purpose underlying your choices, which will increase your spiritual growth. When the same things happen over and over again, your highest Self is trying to get your attention, in essence saying, there is something you need to change, and that something is your mind. The hole in the sidewalk is going to come up again and again and again until you realize that it is a choice you have made. Begin to view those holes in the sidewalk as simply opportunities to choose again.

Chapter Three points out that you must awaken to the fact that you have a choice. It is your responsibility to choose the life you want. In relinquishing that responsibility, you are destined to drift through life aimlessly waiting for others to make your choices for you. Realize that you do not have to choose anger, denial, self-pity or blame. In the past you may have thought you were in pain because of what was done to you, but you now realize that you are in pain because of how you think about what was done to you. To heal, you must come to the realization that you are doing it to yourself. And yes, this is not fun, but ultimately it will set you free.

Even with the knowledge that you have a choice, you can stay just as stuck unless you are willing to exercise that choice. In some ways, knowing that you have a choice and not exercising it is worse because, you may then beat yourself up: 'Now I know I have a choice, but I'm not exercising that choice, I'm just a failure! I'm worthless!' You just fell back into the hole. But now you know that you don't have to stay there.

Personal Empowerment

Once you have grasped the idea that you have a choice, you enter into Chapter Four: *I walk down the street. Again. I see that hole, again! I walk around it.* Personal empowerment is the realization that you have a choice, and then acting on it.

Kahlil Gibran wrote, "You may chain my hands, and shackle my feet; you may even throw me into a dark prison, but you shall not enslave my thinking because it's free."

All too often, we forget that the greatest power we have been given is that of choice. We let people and events enslave us emotionally—I am angry because *you* are doing this to me. Or, I have financial problems because *they* are doing it to me. Or, I have an illness because *God* is doing it to me. In order to attain peace of mind, you must come to recognize that you always have a choice as to how to respond to what is happening in your life.

Blaming anyone or anything for your problems will not set you free. Personal empowerment evolves through recognition that your pain is stemming from how you choose to think about the circumstances in your life. In any situation, you have a choice between imprisonment and freedom. If you created something in your life, you also possess the same creative power to change it. The obstacles, the holes in the sidewalk, are simply opportunities to learn a lesson. Your life is a classroom. You can learn your lessons with the Spirit Within (love) or the ego (fear). Which teacher will you choose?

How do you choose one over the other? Let's say that you are on your way to a family festivity, a business meeting or whatever where you will have to interact with at least one person who pushes your buttons. And so you pray, 'Dear God, I surrender this situation to you because if I don't, my ego is definitely going to lead the way! Please come with me. Guide my thoughts and actions because you and I both know, I can't do this by myself.' Take an instant to choose the teacher of love. If you don't, you've made the choice for the teacher of fear.

Freedom

And so here we are at Chapter Five—Freedom. *I walk down another street*. It is probably fair to say that few of us are there yet, at least in the whole of our lives. But it is your destiny to become free of your self-imposed limitations. *When* is your choice.

One of my favorite lines in *A Course in Miracles* says, *In every difficulty, all distress, and each perplexity the Holy Spirit calls to you and gently says "My brother, choose again"*[11] Don't you love that? "My brother, choose again."

Begin to view the holes in the sidewalk for what they are— opportunities to choose again, to change your mind. You will experience freedom when you stop condemning the world and choose to see it from a higher, more loving vision.

Awareness Exercise

Apply this autobiography to the various aspects of your life. To help you out, I've taken areas many of us struggle with.

❧ Body Issues

Body issues can encompass any number of things: Obsessions about bodily appearance, illness and the like. Projection comes into play with body issues too. The thoughts you hold about yourself are not only projected into your world, but onto your body as well.

With body issues, bring awareness to what you think about yourself. Do you think about how plain, overweight or sick you are? Those are the thoughts that must be brought to the light. Choose again. Ask the Higher Presence to look at your body issues with you. As you begin to change your thoughts, your feelings about yourself will change as well. Your body is not who you are. You are Spirit.

❧ Relationships

For many of us the bugaboo par excellence is relationships. The first half of my life I was stuck in Chapters One and Two. I know it's a cliché, but I realized by the time I was in my 30s that I was choosing emotionally unavailable men. I used to think the concept of choosing unavailable people was absurd! Nevertheless, with awareness I found it was true for me. With much inner work, although I was still attracting them, I recognized it after a few dates and got out of the relationship.

With still more inner work, I progressed to Chapter Four. I still attracted those guys, but I no longer went out with them! Finally, Eureka! Freedom! I made it to Chapter Five! I truly walked down another street when I attracted and chose someone who was emotionally available. In fact, Bill, who is now my husband, also made it to Chapter Five when he chose me because we are the antithesis of each other's type. Have you ever noticed that your type makes you miserable? While stuck in your dysfunctional patterns, you may be attracted to a certain type of person. But as you become emotionally and spiritually healthier, you may find that you are attracted to a completely different type of person.

Seeing yourself in other people doesn't mean that another person isn't really angry, abusive or emotionally unavailable. It doesn't mean they are not doing that, but the empowering question becomes, 'Why am I attracted to it?' I was afraid of love and intimacy. I was unaware that I was emotionally unavailable. When I continued to attract and choose emotionally unavailable people, I was being shown myself. But it always looked like *their* problem, not mine. As it continued to occur in my life, I finally had to recognize that while it may have been their problem, it was also mine.

It is easy to say, "I pick unavailable people," or "I pick

abusive people," or "I pick this or that," but don't get stuck there. Take the next step: 'Yes, I do that, but why? What is this pattern telling me about myself—my fears, denials and blocks?' In order to grow past it, you must look at it closely. Ask for Divine help.

❧ Negative Emotional Patterns

Many of us are stuck in an emotional pattern: Self-pity, anger, guilt, martyrdom, etc. Mine was anger. I recognize that I have not reached Chapter Five. If I had, I would never again choose anger. I'm not there yet! But I am on the border of Chapter Four. I walk in, I see the conflict and although I may still fall into it, I get out immediately! Frequently, I walk into a conflict and realize, 'Wait a minute! I can choose peace instead of this. I can choose happiness instead of choosing to be right. I can walk around the hole in the sidewalk.' I have noticed that I don't attract conflict as often as I once did and when I do, I choose again. Growth comes with recognition that we can make another choice. This does not happen overnight, but steady progress is the path to freedom.

Everything Has a Purpose

Life really does become more fun and meaningful when you do this inner work. You begin to see that there is meaning within all that happens to you. Have you had the experience of going through a divorce, business failure, an illness or whatever, and in the aftermath, realizing that you had gained a gift from the experience? But what would you have thought if you heard, "If you were willing to go through a messy, horrible divorce, it will be okay because you will discover a whole new life for yourself." Or, "If you are willing to go through a life-threatening illness, you will learn what a gift your life is to yourself and others." Apply this idea to any other negative situations you can think of. Would you have said to God, "No way!" Maybe we don't get to know the future because God knows we wouldn't want to go there! But through spiritual practice, you can learn to find the gift in your pain and cease being a victim of it.

We have all experienced those situations when we said, "I know one of these days I will laugh about this!" *Laugh now!* What is keeping you from laughing now when you know you'll be laughing later? It's a choice. You can laugh now. But does that mean that you deny your feelings, invalidate them, or act like you're not hurt? No! Feel bad! Cry! Moan to all your friends! But in a few days, start laughing. Choose again, make another choice—a higher choice. Your choices can liberate you or keep you in bondage.

The journey is about self-realization. It's a long process. You are not seeking human perfection, but wholeness. See your projections as a gift, as a thought process that can teach you whether you are choosing fear or love. With awareness, you can then make another choice—a choice to extend love into the world rather than project fear.

Go back to the autobiography. Look at your issues. Bring awareness to where you are stuck, and look at how far you've come. Call attention to all the positives that you have created in your life. Applaud yourself for that. This is *your* life. Do you want to experience freedom?

And so, as you go about your life and find yourself tempted to fall into that hole yet again, stop for a moment, enter the silence, and listen as the Holy Spirit whispers, "Choose another street."

"I AM GOOD ENOUGH!"

Most of us have felt like a failure at some point in our lives, and if not a failure, then at least unworthy, unlovable or not good enough. These feelings are not based on truth, but on our mistaken interpretations of who and what we are. Nothing you do, think or achieve is necessary to establish your worth. Your worth has already been established—by God. *This point is not debatable.*

To return to the remembrance of this truth, you chose to come to a place (earth) where the predominant thought system is one of fear, limitation and "there's not enough!" The challenge is to live amidst such a thought system and come to remember that you are not a being of fear and limitation, but one of abundance, love, creativity and strength.

Moreover, if earth were a place where you felt continually secure, loved and validated, there would be no challenge. Spiritual growth is a continual movement toward remembering that nothing outside of you can provide the security, love and validation you crave. It must be cultivated within. Just as the heroes in all the great stories and myths challenged the thought system of their world, so too, must you.

"Challenge" means to call in question or to arouse. In order to be a hero in your own life, you must first call in question everything you currently believe about yourself, and thus arouse the remembrance of your true worth.

Most of our beliefs, even the grandiose ones, were created from an ego-driven, fear-filled thought system. A belief cannot be corrected with the same thought system that created it. Take your erroneous evaluations of yourself to a higher thought system where they can be corrected: 'Dear God, reveal to me my mistaken beliefs so that I might know who I really am.' Once you sincerely say such a prayer, *pay attention* because the prayer will be answered.

Healing is a process that continues throughout your life. Once you ask God to heal you, you will be guided to the people and ideas that will facilitate that healing. In fact, your Spirit put this book in your hands. With examination of the beliefs, attitudes and thoughts that might have contributed to your feelings of being unworthy or not good enough, you will come to recognize that a new perception can heal your life.

Say "The End" To Your Story

You might feel unworthy because of a story you have continued to tell yourself, and thus have come to believe. Your story begins: Once upon a time, someone, somewhere, told you in words and/or actions that you were not good enough. And you believed them! At that point, you began to live your story rather than your life.

The plot involves victimization usually not from just one person, but various people and situations. Your story is about the past. If you dwell on the fact that you were victimized in some way, you will continue to attract similar situations throughout your life. Viewing life through the lens of your story (the past) only keeps you stuck there. This recognition is not to invalidate painful experiences, rather, it validates that we all share the same story, albeit in different forms.

There was a period in my life when my past erupted into my present. I felt anger and despair. For the first time, at age thirty-three, I began to tell my story to a few close friends and a therapist.

The more I told my story, the easier it was and the better I felt about it. Telling my story at that point in my life was necessary for healing. I no longer tell my story, however, because I no longer need to. Continuing to tell it would only impede my spiritual growth, not facilitate it.

There is a profound difference between telling your story for the purpose of healing, versus telling it to blame or excuse the current state of your life. As long as you think that you are being treated a certain way because of a handicap, your race, gender, religion (insert your own), you do not have to look at yourself and can thereby continue to blame others, the devil or God for your problems and difficulties. You can break free of self-imposed imprisonment with the willingness to give up your story—the excuses for the state of your life.

We have forgotten who and what we really are, and have therefore made up excuses and stories to justify what we are not. You are not an innocent victim. The question becomes, do you want to move forward in your life or do you want to continue to blame someone or something for why your life isn't fulfilling now?

It's time to give up your story and get on with the living of your life. It is only through the willingness to forgive all the characters in your story (and this includes yourself) that you can finally say, "The End." Forgiveness becomes an easier process with understanding that the people from the past whom you feel have hurt you, also suffered from deep-seated feelings of unworthiness—they have a story too.

Our stories can imprison us or they can set us free to be more loving and compassionate people. Consider that your story didn't happen to you, but for you. Once you find the gift in your story, you can break out of self-imposed imprisonment and move on to living a meaningful and powerful life.

Comparison Thinking

You can feel not good enough when you compete with and compare yourself to others. I know a man who earns several hundred thousand dollars a year, but because he compares himself to his brother who earns millions, he feels like a failure. So here we have someone who, at least financially, is more successful than most people but based on his mistaken perceptions, he feels like a failure.

When you attempt to feel worthy by comparing yourself to others, it will never work because there will always be someone who is wealthier, better looking, smarter, or whatever. When you indulge in comparison thinking, some days you feel better than other people and some days you come up short, but still, you are left with the feeling of not being good enough.

I love what May Sarton had to say about it: *You have to dare to be yourself, however frightening or strange that self may prove to be.* Willingness to stand up and be who you are, *is* frightening because let's face it, you probably haven't done that before. Initially, it is a strange experience but a liberating one as well.

One of the greatest gifts I have gained from spiritual practice is that I have come to like who I am. No, not every minute or even every day, but I have an overall sense of being a worthy and valuable human being. As long as you hang out with your ego self, you will depend on other people to make you feel validated and worthwhile. Other people cannot give you validation because they are looking for you to give it to them. We are all in this together.

Midlife Assessments

There are two big disappointments in life: (1) not getting what you want, and (2) getting it. Someone once told me that he was depressed because he thought that by this time in his life (50s) he would be established; he would be set in life. In the prior year, he had gone through a divorce, a business failure and the death of a parent.

And then someone else told me that he was depressed because, "All of my life I've made goals, and I've achieved every one of them. I'm depressed because I don't know what new goals to make." His depression probably stemmed from thinking that having achieved his goals, he would be happy. But he wasn't happy, so what now?

Here we have two people: One got what he wanted, the other didn't. They are both depressed. It is interesting to note that the man who was depressed because his life hadn't turned out the way he wanted it to, is now going to therapy and seeking higher truth. The other person is still doing the same thing, setting goals and achieving them and then setting them at higher levels. He is still running around in circles like a hamster on a wheel.

At or about midlife, I suspect that many of us could relate to one of these two people. From childhood, most of us have been taught that our worthiness comes from worldly achievement of one kind or another. So we live at least the first half of our lives, predominately as an ego: Caught up in fear, survival and establishing a personal identity.

Each of the aforementioned men was experiencing a midlife crisis—*Is this all there is*? Carl Jung observed that a midlife crisis is really a spiritual crisis; and that any problem we have after age thirty-five is in fact, a spiritual one.

"Crisis" is a turning point; a condition of instability that leads to decisive change. Midlife can be a turning point because we often do not enter spiritual maturity until we have lived many years thinking that we had all the answers. Keep in mind that thirty-five is an arbitrary number. At about that age I experienced my personal midlife crisis but for others it might be earlier or later in their life span—if at all.

What occurs during these periods is a condition of instability that can lead to recognition that perhaps there is a better way to live your life than the way you have been living it. For some, the better way might be seeking higher truth about who they are and their place in the world. For others, the better way might be to continue looking for more and better in the world. Midlife can ultimately serve to take you to a new level of purpose and meaning in your life.

Enjoy Today

True overnight success takes fifteen years—at least! You may feel like a failure if you don't see the fruits of your labors immediately. The full extension of your gifts and talents requires practice, patience, perseverance, and maturity. When I began lecturing on spirituality, people told me that I was really good at it and would be "out there" in no time. Fortunately, even then, I knew that it would take many years of practice, patience and perseverance to develop the spiritual maturity required to present this material to the world. This recognition helped me enjoy my years of preparation rather than waiting to be happy when.

If you are not enjoying the years leading up to any kind of worldly success—do you really think that you are going to be able to enjoy your success for more than a few weeks, months or years? And then, what do you do next? Write another book? Start another business? Make more money? Marry someone else? Recently I read an interview with a famous actor who said, "It was more fun trying to get to this level of success than it is being there." If you are not enjoying the day-to-day of your present life, what is going to change about you that will enable you to enjoy it later?

On another level, if you cannot enjoy your life until you make more money, lose weight, find a mate, and so on, when "that" gets here you will be waiting for something else to happen before you can enjoy your life. You have probably lived this time and time again.

A patient of mine lost 75 pounds. I asked her if she was enjoying her life more. Her answer was very interesting: "I thought that all my problems were because of my excess weight and when I lost it, at first I was ecstatic. I felt better about myself and I had more self-confidence, but it wasn't long before I realized that I still had all the same problems. This experience has made me aware that just because you fix the outside doesn't mean that you have fixed the inside. I'm still waiting for that something else to make me happy."

This is not to discount feeling enjoyment about your accomplishments. But your accomplishments won't pinch hit for an inner sense of self-worth, or solve your problems. As you begin to develop a relationship with that worthy and good enough part of yourself, you will begin to enjoy the process of living your life. Even as you desire to improve or change certain aspects of your life, a sense of self-acceptance can facilitate those changes.

You Cannot Avoid Mistakes

Someone told me that all during her life she had worked really hard not to step in any messes. If you want to live a joyous and purposeful life, you are not going to avoid them. The people we admire and respect have all stepped in messes. The reason we admire them, however, is because they not only stepped away, but also made something beautiful out of it.

We frequently learn much more from our failures and mistakes than we ever learn from our successes. Perhaps you have made mistakes in the financial arena, but through those experiences have learned how to live more abundantly. Through making mistakes in relationships, you may now have learned how to have relationships built on love and trust. Through numerous dieting failures, you may now have learned to forgo dieting and trust your body's signals. After bringing awareness and responsibility to your negative emotional patterns, you may now have learned to choose love, forgiveness and peace. Every experience can provide an opportunity for growth and healing.

How Do You Define Success?

Some of our greatest successes we have judged as failure, and some of our biggest failures were evaluated as success. Take time to reflect on and perhaps write about the times when you felt that you had failed. Did any advantages come out of those experiences? Did you learn anything about yourself? If you learned anything through those experiences, then you are a success.

Next, reflect on the aspects of your life that you evaluate as successful. Did you make a lot of money, attain the perfect body, a high profile, and the like; all the while alienating yourself from your family and friends? Does the world tell you that you are successful, but your heart tells you otherwise?

Our ideas of success often have to do with how much money we have, what we own, how we look or what we drive. We aspire to be on a new version of that old TV show, "Lifestyles of the Rich and Famous" because in our society, we have equated monetary success with personal worth. After all, as Robert Roskind points out in his book *In The Spirit of Business*, we are not going to see a TV show called, "Lifestyles of the Balanced and Loving."

There is nothing wrong with having money or any kind of worldly success unless you let it, or the lack thereof, define who you are. Success is really about attaining a sense of inner peace while enjoying your life. Redefining your ideas of success and failure can bring you to a new level of peace and enjoyment.

The Road to Success Is Paved With Failure

Thomas Edison said, "I failed my way to success." He failed many times before he discovered the light bulb. Just as he discovered the light bulb through learning from his numerous mistakes and failures, you too, discover the light within you as you learn through your numerous mistakes and failures. Although, when it comes to failure, please understand that you cannot really fail. You can only grow. There is no such thing as failure, only lessons to be learned. So you didn't learn the lesson this time around, it will come around again. Fear of failure can limit you. We all make mistakes. But we must learn from them and then move on. I've heard author, Marianne Williamson say that the sign of a great person is not someone who never falls down, greatness lies in how they get up.

Anyone who has done anything of value has almost always been rejected, felt not good enough and made mistakes. Joey Green's book, *The Road to Success Is Paved With Failure* gives us a few examples:

John Grishim's first novel, *A Time to Kill* was rejected by 16 agents and a dozen publishing companies. Winwood Press published 5,000 copies in 1989 but sales were dismal.

F. D. Roosevelt ran for president of the United States in 1920 on the Democratic ticket. He lost. The following year he was stricken with polio and his legs became paralyzed. He went on to be elected governor of New York in 1928; President of the United States in 1932, 1936, 1940 and 1944.

Elvis Presley's music teacher at L. C. Humes High School in Memphis Tennessee gave him a C and told him that he couldn't sing.

A nun stuffed Bruce Springsteen into a garbage can when he was in the third grade because, "she told me that was where I belonged!"

And my favorite—Bill Gates dropped out of Harvard in 1975. Thank you Bill!

These examples serve to show us that sometimes what the world defines as success or failure is not necessarily an assessment of our lives. I read somewhere that the only time you can't afford to fail is the last time you try. My motto is *never give up*! Everything you go through is preparation to do what you came here to do.

I once gave a poster to my son that spoke dramatically about what was happening to him. *Courage is daring to take that first step, or a different path. It is the decision to place your dreams above your fears.* Courage has nothing to do with being unafraid, but everything to do with doing it anyway.

What Is Right About You?

Not only is the belief that you are not good enough, or don't deserve rooted in the things you don't like about yourself, but it is also rooted in your refusal to recognize the things that *are* right about you. Once you have accepted a certain level of personal responsibility, you may start with, "I've created all this negative stuff in my life. Oh, I'm such a sinner, I'm so bad!" STOP! In your acceptance of yourself as unworthy and not good enough, you think that your evaluation of yourself is truer than God's evaluation of you.

Look back on your life—and realize that you have created much more that is positive and beautiful than negative. You may not think this to be true because you've only focused on the negative. Have you ever brought awareness and attention to what is right about you? There is much beauty within you that has been left unacknowledged. So why see only the ugly stuff? You can talk about your negative patterns, you can talk about how deep and dark they are, but can you talk about the gold in you? Carl Jung observed that even if you really trust someone, you will resist to the nth degree telling him or her about the gold in you. Why?

Once you start talking about the inner gold, people give you that look which seems to say, "Who do you think you are? You're not good enough, let me tell ya!" And you believe them!

Character Assassination

Our culture has fallen into character assassination, especially toward successful and public people. Is there anything in your past that you would not want exposed to the world? And if it were exposed, does that invalidate all the positive aspects accomplished in your life? Anyone you admire and respect has also failed, felt not good enough and made mistakes. It seems that we are always looking for what someone may have done wrong, forgetting that their mistakes led them to where they are now—someone with something to say.

Character assassination doesn't just hurt the people we attack, it hurts all of society because it silences those who have light to extend to the world who can become afraid to extend it. Due to the prevalence of such criticism and assassination, when I began speaking and writing on spirituality, I was afraid of getting my work published. I've grown since then. I came to realize that I might be invalidated, turned down and criticized, but by God I have something to say that will benefit others, and I am going to stand up and say it.

Have you been withholding your gifts to the world out of fear of recrimination? It helps to understand that the attacks are not personal, but rather directed to the light. However, if there are not enough people willing to shine their light and extend their gifts, despite criticism, then where does that leave us? The great thing is that as a society we have a short attention span. Just keep extending your light. The media visible people are not letting criticism stop them, so why are you letting it stop you on a less visible level?

If You Don't Try, You Can't Succeed

If you don't try, you can't fail. But if you don't try, you can't succeed either. The irony is that we are afraid of failing because people will tear us down, and we are afraid of succeeding because people will also tear us down. So why not extend your light and let them try to tear you down for that. It's a no-lose situation because you will be living a happy and meaningful life. As you come forth with your light, you will attract more of that same energy to you. Some people will be disturbed by it, but so many more will be helped by your willingness to extend your gifts to the world.

You are meant to live a life of magnitude. The energy of goodness and love flows within you and around you, but it is blocked with I'm-a-failure thinking. It is time to get over it because, the world not only needs you—*you need you*! You need the you that comes from that powerful place you've been denying.

Are You Using Your Gifts?

We have all been given gifts and talents. Are you not using them because someone called you a failure or said that you weren't good enough? We've said that to ourselves! The people who are really going for it out there are the people who, on some level said, "That's not true for me! It's not true that I didn't have the right education. It's not true that I'm not the right gender. It's not true that I'm not the right race. It's not true that I'm not attractive enough, thin enough, smart enough … It's not true! It might be true for you, but it's not true for me because I'm not buying it."

What you believe about yourself becomes your reality. "Look at all this evidence," you can state. What you believe about yourself becomes true in your life. And based on that self-perception, you see the erroneous evidence proving that you are right.

Return to the Truth

So what happened? How did we become so mixed up, fear-filled and confused about who and what we are? Once upon a time, we forgot to love. We forgot that love was our true nature, and embraced fear instead. Now is the time to return to the fact, the truth, and the remembrance that we are love. Once upon a time, we used our free will to step out of the natural harmony of the universe—it is now time to step back in. Once upon a time, we forgot that we are created from a Source of light, love and abundance, and it is now time to return to that remembrance. Once upon a time, we bought into the idea that we were weak, limited and just not good enough. Now is the time to instill in our mind that we are powerful, unlimited and always *good enough!*

Spiritual Practice

We return to the remembrance of who and what we are through spiritual practice: Meditation, prayer, extending love and forgiveness, and bringing awareness to our negative patterns and tendencies. Be willing to cultivate a practice of sitting down and communing with your Self. The energy in this universe that is powerful, perfect and complete rests within you. Are you willing to claim it?

No Enemy Except Yourself

You have no enemy except yourself. Your only enemy is your failure to recognize who you really are. You are a creation of Love. And yes, it's hard to remember that in this world. Every day I choose to deal with my negative patterns. But while the other me was stuck in those patterns, the present me can choose against them. And of course, sometimes I fall into them. But where the old was lost in the darkness, I now have solid tools in prayer and meditation to help bring me back to the truth.

Are you willing to own and use what you have available to you? Sit down *tonight* and write a list of the things that are right about you. And don't forget to include all the positive and beautiful things you have created in your life. And then write down all the junk you have created. Everyone has ugly stuff—most of us have a lot of it. You need to look at that too. But be willing to look at what is good and right you. Acknowledge the beauty you have created.

Willingness Is Everything

Ultimately the decision is made by your willingness. You create a better life through your willingness. You may think that you don't deserve to be happy, but are you willing to be? You may think that you cannot forgive that person who totally screwed up your life, but are you willing to? You may think that you don't deserve to live a powerful, fulfilling, happy life, but are you willing to? Are you willing? Affirm: 'I am now willing to receive, accept and allow God's healing into every facet of my life.' Affirm it until you believe it.

Your Task

May you decide on this day to create something new, to begin again—to stand forth differently than you have in the past. Seek to heal old wounds with family, friends and others who have touched your life. Dare to love more fully, forgive more freely, appreciate more deeply and serve with more compassion. Easier said than done of course, but this is your task. Ultimately, it doesn't matter what you own, accomplish, or save—what matters is whether or not you love.

And so, as you go about your life, become willing to open your heart and extend your gifts. You are needed. You are significant. You make a difference. Even if no one else thinks that you're good enough, but you do—then that's enough! Begin now to fulfill your task, which will culminate in a glorious, well lived life.

HAPPINESS IS A CHOICE

Happiness—the eternal quest. We long to be happy. We strive to be happy. We think that everyone else is happier than we are! Over the years, I have asked people if they are happy and have received all kinds of answers:

"I will be happy when I have the things I want (a romantic relationship, a great job, etc.)".

"I was happy, but I lost it when (divorce, illness, financial problems, etc.)".

"I am happy because I have everything I want, but I have to admit that I am often afraid of losing what I have."

"Is anyone happy?"

"I will be happy when I win the lottery!"

"How do I know? What is happiness anyway?"

Although there are many possible answers, these examples represent how most of us would respond to the question. Perhaps the most telling response is "How do I know? What is happiness anyway?"

We generally think of happiness as a state of well-being or euphoria, or some other state we have yet to experience. During years of spiritual practice, I have come to experience happiness as inner peace. In truth, happiness is not something we can attain from the outside world; rather it is a state of consciousness that can only be found within. Once we come to this awareness, we find that no matter what is happening in our lives we can still be happy. We discover that happiness does not require people or circumstances to be a certain way.

When you woke up this morning, what was the context of your thoughts? Did you face the day filled with worry, anxiety or fear? Or did you wake up with an appreciation for who you are and what you have? Arising with an attitude of appreciation and hopefulness will extend a much lighter energy than fretting over bills or dwelling on what or who has done you wrong.

Happiness is a choice. But before we can choose happiness, we must first bring awareness to what we choose instead. Self-pity, judgment, anger and fear are obstacles to happiness. Once you recognize these states of mind, you can make a choice as to whether or not to indulge them. Much of your inner work involves paying attention to how you react and respond to the people and situations that confront you every day.

Do You Want To Be Happy Or Right?

So much of our unhappiness stems from the need to be right about the people we meet and the events that occur. Some of the ways we hold onto being right is in our beliefs that:

- There are no good men/women out there.
- There aren't enough jobs.
- People are up to no good.
- I'm too old.
- He/she started it.
- There's not enough money.
- I don't have the right education.
- (Insert your own.)

When we cling to such self-limiting beliefs they adhere to us as our reality. We then think that we are right about the world but even so, we're still not happy. We have a choice. We can hold onto limiting beliefs, or we can challenge them and choose happiness.

The state of your life has everything to do with how you think. Happiness requires a changed perception. You can change your perceptions only after you have brought awareness to them and their effects in your life. Through this practice, you recognize that happiness truly is a choice, and that you must again and again bring awareness to how you choose against it.

The Blame Game

Why do we blame other people or situations for our unhappiness? Simple, it's easier than taking a deeper look at us. All too often, we project our negative patterns onto other people. We see "them" as hurting or victimizing us when, in reality, we use other people to hurt ourselves.

Most of us have experienced being told something hurtful, or having things said about us that weren't true. And conversely, we have probably done the same thing to others. Was it really about them? No. Our words or actions were a projection of the condemnation we felt toward ourselves, if only in that moment. Happiness comes through stopping in such moments, and reflecting on the truth about the situation. The truth is that we relate, react and respond to other people and situations based on how we feel about ourselves.

When we blame others for our problems, when we take from others and avoid responsibility, we are unhappy. When we do or say something mean or thoughtless, in not wanting to face our own culpability, we seek to find something wrong with "them" to justify our behavior. Blaming other people absolves us from having to look within and thus drives us further from happiness.

Forgiveness Is the Key to Happiness

Your purpose here is to learn forgiveness. As you fulfill that purpose you will be happy. Every time you choose whether or not to forgive, you are really choosing whether or not to be happy. Forgiving those who you perceive as the cause of unhappiness sets you free from your victim stance in the world. Forgiveness is the key that opens the door to heaven here on earth. Everything that occurs gives you an opportunity to make the choice of forgiveness.

Happiness and forgiveness are not only your purpose, but also your responsibility. When you are sad, angry or upset, you affect other people. But, you do not affect them positively. When you are living a happy and peaceful life, you automatically share that with others and thus fulfill the purpose and function you came here to fulfill.

No Melodrama in Happiness

Have you ever noticed that you don't talk on the phone as much when life is going well? And when it isn't, you are always on the phone. I was on the phone for hours with my girlfriends, especially during the dating phase of my life—our constant lament being, "Ain't it awful!" There is no melodrama in happiness. The problem for many of us is that we get stuck in the dramatic scenarios of our lives. We look at everything from the most negative viewpoint possible and then talk about it ad nauseam!

As your growth progresses, you may find that you attract new friends and often leave behind many old ones. Just as a recovered alcoholic may have to avoid former drinking buddies, you must sometimes let go of those who prefer to stay stuck in the drama of unhappiness. If some of your relationships are based on the mutual lament of how bad things are, if you are both card carrying members of the "Ain't It Awful Club," it may be time to re-evaluate that relationship. This process usually occurs naturally because he or she won't want to talk to you once your reply becomes, "Well maybe it isn't so awful." Those who are now on the forty-fifth installment of the same problem aren't going to want to hear, "Well maybe it's time you gave that one up." Some relationships grow as you do, building on a new foundation, and others must simply be left behind.

Of course, the problems in our lives need to be talked about in order to gain insight, clarity and objectivity. We all need those close friends with whom we can be vulnerable. I so value the friendships where we are not only able to talk about the drama, but spend even more time talking about the transcendence of it. It's not that we don't commiserate about the darkness, but by the end of the conversation we have embraced the light. We remind each other of the spiritual principles that will help turn the situation around, or help us experience peace in the midst of it.

Make Another Choice

In his book, *Notes On How to Live in the World and Still Be Happy*, Hugh Prather uses the example of diarrhea. If you were talking to someone and suddenly had an attack of diarrhea, what would you do? The answer is obvious. How does this apply to choosing happiness? Let's say that you are in the midst of a family gathering and become angry toward someone there. You can think, 'Oh my God! Diarrhea!' and excuse yourself. Believe it or not, this can be a great spiritual practice because it can remind you that you have another choice. You can remain present, or you can excuse yourself and run to the bathroom, and while there—pray! Don't give other people the power to rule your state of mind. Choose peace.

Any moment you can stop and ask yourself, 'Am I at peace?' If not, bring awareness to who or what you are thinking about. If you are thinking thoughts of anger, judgment or self-pity—there's the reason you are not at peace. In those moments I frequently affirm, 'I can see peace instead of this,' or 'Peace to my mind, my thoughts are still.' Happiness truly is a choice. In any instant we can choose peace or conflict.

A patient once said that she really liked coming to me because I am such a genuinely happy person. I laughed and said, "Follow me around all day!" While at work I make a decision to be happy. I take my role as a doctor seriously. It wouldn't be helpful to my patients if I were miserable. Reflecting on that one day, I came to the profound realization that I could also be happy at the grocery store, on the freeway, or anywhere I happen to be. It's a choice. Happiness is a great choice to make!

Happiness In The Midst Of Problems
Even in the midst of your problems you can choose happiness. Within a problem you can remain fearful, worried or anxious, or you can use it to bring you closer to God. Try this prayer:

> *Dear God,*
> *Faced with this problem,*
> *I know not how to respond to it.*
> *I know only that I cannot use the past*
> *to guide me now.*
> *In the past, I used my problems*
> *to feel failure, pain and fear.*
> *I let them become obstacles*
> *to my happiness, and thus*
> *pushed You further from my mind.*
> *In this moment,*
> *I surrender my problem to You.*
> *May it be used*
> *to bring me closer to Your light,*
> *closer to Your love,*
> *closer, dear God,*
> *to You.*

In sincerely saying this prayer, you are refusing to handle your problems the way you have handled them in the past, which may I remind you, did not work. You cannot choose happiness by yourself. But through calling on God (a higher thought system) you indicate your willingness to choose it. God takes it from there as you get out of your own way. Through prayer, you exit a consciousness of fear and anxiety, and enter one of peace and healing.

Note that the aforementioned prayer doesn't ask God to take the problem away. It asks that God bring you closer to love *through* the problem. God cannot take away your problems because God didn't put them there. In the past, my focus on the problem kept me from healing. I now recognize that any problem can be used to bring us closer to love. When you focus on how fat, broke, sick or lonely you are, you have shut God (the energy of healing) out. When you focus on the problem—are you closer to love, are you closer to the light, are you closer to healing or are you farther away? Peace is attained through recognition that any problem can be seen as a stepping stone to God rather than as an obstacle.

If you are in any way spiritual, you may wonder why God isn't seeing your good works, hearing your prayers and thus removing the problems from your life. Many people embark on a spiritual path thinking their problems will disappear—at least I did. When I started the one year process of the workbook of *A Course in Miracles*, I thought that by the time I finished it all of my problems would be solved. Ha! After 14 months I finished it, only to find that some of my problems were worse than ever! But the gift was that I was at peace within them. The power inherent in the practice of spiritual principles lies not in the absence of problems, but more profoundly, in a sense of peace in the midst of them. Problems are not going to go away, but your pain around them can.

Be willing to delve into the inner depths so that the cause of your problems can be revealed. Call on God to help you do that.

Problems can be seen as opportunities that facilitate growth. Disciplining your mind to think this way can help you avert problems, or experience their transcendence as you seek the gift within them. We've all heard, "Behind every cloud lies a silver lining." In truth, God provides the silver lining, *we* provide the cloud!

As you do this inner work, you begin to experience a greater sense of peace and happiness. And then, lo and behold, another obstacle comes up: 'Uh Oh! What's going to happen next?' It seems that even in our happiness, we wait for the other shoe to drop. This kind of thinking is just the ego calling us back to fear. You can choose against the ego by saying, "Thank you for sharing your anxiety with me, now get lost!"

Happiness is a choice. If you're honest with yourself, so is pain. You may have the erroneous idea that happiness is the avoidance of pain. But when you learn to embrace the whole of your life, the joy and the pain, you recognize that pain also has value. Physical or emotional pain indicates that something is not right within you. If you deny or repress it, the pain worsens. Become willing to look at your pain, embrace it even—ask your pain what it is trying to tell you.

Although emotional pain is an inevitable part of life, its purpose is to teach you that you can live without pain. Pain is inevitable until you recognize that you can replace it with peace. But if you walk around with your newfound spiritual principles saying, "I don't have any problems, I'm spiritual now," that is not transcendence of pain, but avoidance and denial. If someone stabs you in the back (of the betrayal variety) and you don't initially feel pain that is again denial, not transcendence. Pain may be inevitable in this world, but whether you hold onto it for six days, six months, or six years, is a choice only you can make.

The Problem of More

There are other obstacles to happiness. In his book, *Happiness is a Serious Problem*, Dennis Prager wrote that he had seen the following ad: "If you are not completely satisfied with your sex life, give us a call." He realized that it was the words "completely satisfied" that made the ad so brilliant. He imagined ads that said, if you are not completely satisfied with your children, your financial status, your house, or your toothpaste—give us a call. His point, are we ever *completely satisfied* with anything? It seems that we always want more, and we want more—abundantly!

Speaking of more, many people feel if they had more money their problems would be solved. I read about a psychologist who was asked if he would rather counsel rich people or poor people. "Rich people," he replied, "because they already know that money won't solve their problems." Money cannot make you happy; however, it can make you unhappy—if you allow it to. How often do we let money or the lack of it, destroy our happiness?

A study of people who had won the lottery revealed that after a certain number of years, every single one of the winners were in exactly the same financial situation as before they won the money, and some were even worse off. Many wished they had never won it.

An excess of money symbolizes freedom. With a lot of extra money we can: escape a difficult situation that we're in; enjoy the situation that we're in more fully; or create an altogether new situation. But what are we really looking for? Freedom. It's not that we necessarily want to take cruises for the rest of our lives; we want to escape from where we are. But just as money cannot bring happiness, it cannot give freedom either. Freedom, like happiness, is an internal affair. Recognizing that on a deep level is like winning the lottery.

Having the things that money can buy can be great fun. But if in your pursuit of money you lose the things it can't buy, you will be unhappy. You experience happiness concerning money when you can come to enjoy and appreciate the benefits of it without coming from a state of need, lack and scarcity.

Getting "things" may seem important, yet when you reflect on when you have felt happiest, it probably came from the acts of love, friendship and compassion that you gave to others and received. Expectations of what money, things, situations or people can do for you, blocks your ability to enjoy what is actually occurring in your life.

Have you ever thought that when you got a certain thing, you'd be happy? And then you got it, and you were happy—for a few days, weeks or even months. Nevertheless, it wasn't long before you returned to that feeling of something's missing. This feeling has haunted many of us throughout our lives.

We may think that what is missing stems from whatever we don't have or didn't get. 'I would be happy if only, or I'll be happy when ...' The inner void cannot be filled by anything outside of you. It must be filled from within.

Do You Feel Unlovable?

Another way happiness can seem elusive is in feeling that we are unlovable. The problem for many human beings is that at our core, we feel that we are unworthy of love. We find it hard to believe that a God we can't see can love us when we don't even believe that those we can see love us.

Unconditional love is not only something we cannot imagine receiving from another human being, we also can't imagine extending it. A friend told me the only person she had experienced unconditional love with was her son. Reflecting on that, I realized that I have experienced that with my stepson. There is nothing he could do that would make me not love him. And he's tested it a lot! I cannot imagine not loving him. Don't you think that most of our parents felt that way about us? It may not have looked like it, might not have felt like it, but I think most parents feel unconditional love for their children. This doesn't mean that we don't get angry with our children, but we love them no matter what.

We don't believe God loves us unconditionally. We don't believe God loves us with total acceptance, yet we do it with our children. If we flawed human beings can unconditionally love our children, don't you think that God, the energy of perfect love, can unconditionally love you despite whatever sins you think you have committed? When we equate our love for our children with God's love for us, how could we be unhappy?

Another analogy for God's love is found in the love we feel toward our pets. I am a dog lover. My dogs make me believe in a benevolent and loving God. It's as if God looked onto the world and said, "Those humans just cannot figure out how to love each other. They need an example!" Our pets don't care about how we look, how much money we make, or about our race, gender or sexuality—they simply love us unconditionally. And that is why we love them. Again, that is God's relationship to you. Take that in. Be willing to let God's love become a reality in your life.

We find this hard to do because on a spiritual level, we are all handicapped. We have forgotten that love is in and around us. And that is our handicap. So often, we are blind to the many gifts that already embrace our lives. And we are deaf to the ever present calls for love.

Due to an illness, Helen Keller became blind and deaf at a very young age. Through the loving tutelage of her teacher, Annie Sullivan, she returned to her senses so to speak. Jean Houston, in her book *Public Like A Frog*, wrote about her meeting with this incredible woman when her 4th grade class went to visit her:

Helen talked with us, and then asked the class if there were any questions. I raised my hand and as Helen scanned my face with her hands I blurted out, 'Why are you so happy?'

Helen laughed and laughed and then replied, 'My child, I am so happy because I live each day as though it was my last, and life in all its moments is so full of glory.'

Through this encounter Jean experienced Helen's radiance firsthand, and said that she has never been the same since.

Live Fully Today

Happiness is found in the moment, in living each day as though it were all you had. A life well lived is not lived in the past or in the future, but in the moment. We all know we are going to die. Not knowing how or when is so frightening to many of us that, on an unconscious level, we don't truly live the life we are meant to live. But may I remind you—there will always be a tomorrow. Whether you enter tomorrow in physical form or in spirit, may it enter your consciousness *today* that everything is right exactly as it is. Grow to live in trust that this is a benevolent and loving universe, governed by a benevolent and loving God. Returning to the remembrance of this truth is the purpose of life here on earth.

With that understanding, may you resolve to appreciate the many blessings that have embraced your life. May you come to recognize each new day as a gift, a present—wrapped just for you. For that is what it is. Every person you meet, each event that occurs carries an opportunity to love and be loved, to forgive and to be forgiven, to serve and to be served.

And so, as you go about your life, may you remember that as you give, you receive. Be willing to let your very life be a demonstration of love. In so doing, you fulfill your highest potential, your most beautiful destiny, and have cause to finally say, *I am happy*.

3 SPIRITUAL PRACTICE

The aim of life is to live,
and to live means to be aware.
Joyously, drunkenly, serenely,
divinely aware!

– Henry Miller

A person's mind may be likened
to a garden, which may be
intelligently cultivated or allowed
to run wild; but whether cultivated
or neglected, it must, and will
bring forth.

– James Allen, As a Man Thinketh

I began taking piano lessons in my late 30s. The hardest part about it was that I had to practice every day. And that's the hardest part about spiritual work—we have to practice every day. We live in a quick-fix society and we want our spiritual growth to occur in that same quick-fix fashion. It doesn't work like that. We can read, study and memorize spiritual precepts, but if we don't apply what we've learned to everyday situations, nothing in our lives will change. Spiritual growth requires practice, patience and perseverance.

This chapter will focus on growth as a three-step process: Awareness, responsibility, and forgiveness. To gain deeper understanding, the steps will be applied to four spiritual laws:

- Love One Another
- What Goes Around Comes Around
- Do It Now or Do It Later
- There's No Free Lunch!

A law is a rule that must be obeyed; a principle based on the predictable consequences of an act or condition. All societies, religions, governments, etc. establish rules that must be obeyed. But these rules often vary from one place or structure to the next. Spiritual laws, however, apply to each one of us—equally. You will not be divinely punished for noncompliance with spiritual laws because universal laws are always fair and work only for good.

When you choose to live in accordance with them, you experience a happier and more purposeful life.

LAW ONE

Love One Another

The first and most important universal law is *Love one another.* While driving to work one day, it occurred to me that this law is applicable to the most basic law of traffic control: Stop at the red light and go on the green. If we don't comply with this basic law our streets will be filled with chaos, confusion, violence and death. When we don't abide by the law *Love one another* our world is filled with chaos, confusion, violence and death. Have you watched the news lately? The news reflects the extreme consequences of our failure to love one another. To a lesser extreme, although certainly more prevalent are the consequences experienced in our daily lives.

We have been told to love other people as we love ourselves. Well we do—when you consider that we don't love ourselves all that much. So the first step in the practice of this law is to bring awareness and responsibility to your thoughts, and how they influence your capacity to love other people and yourself.

Being aware of your thoughts, however, does not automatically assume responsibility for them. You may be alert to the fact that you're angry, but have blamed the cause onto your spouse, the IRS, your co-workers or whatever. Thus, you have not taken responsibility for your anger, but have instead made someone or something responsible.

Think of responsibility this way: If I want to sell my neighbor's car, I can't because I don't own my neighbor's car. But if I did own it, I could sell it, give it away, trade it in or keep it. Well, it's the same with our thoughts.

Let's say that you become aware that you're angry. Then what? There are several options: You can give it away by blaming someone else; you can keep it and let it stew inside of you, or you can trade it in for a higher understanding. But until you own what is yours, you can't do anything with it.

If you were to bring awareness to your thoughts for even a day, you might recognize resentment as a dominant theme. Most of us are not conscious of the resentments we harbor toward other people. Ask the Inner Spirit to make you aware of your resentments. This is important because resentment is poisonous. Not only can it precipitate physical and emotional illness; resentment also hinders your ability to love by keeping you stuck in the past with a continual focus on who has done you wrong. In addition, it impedes manifestation of abundance, and the extension of your inherent creative gifts into the world.

With awareness, you can learn to use your resentments as spiritual practice. Try this exercise: Make a list of a few people whom you resent. With each one, ask yourself what feeling or emotion they trigger: Anger? Rejection? Unworthiness? Self-pity? Also, what aspect of your life do they comment on: Your work? Parenting? Relationships? Personality?

Awareness can help you see that perhaps their comments are triggering your own feelings of unworthiness. The critical and judgmental comments made by others can really get to you when feeling insecure about particular areas in your life. Asking these questions can alert you to the fact that your reactions have to do with you, not other people. Inner work is about becoming aware of and working through those vulnerable places within us.

Return to the Truth

I once saw a cartoon that said, *Here stands the adult child of a perfect parent*. No one was there! There aren't any perfect parents. Nevertheless, many parents repeatedly have their defenses triggered because it is an area where other people freely offer advice and criticism. Especially those people who don't have kids! We may feel even more vulnerable if our child is experiencing a particular difficulty.

I felt especially insecure in this area when I became a parent to my husband's nine-year-old son. Being a good parent for him is something I consciously worked on, but even so, I was not immune to criticism. Ironically, something he said when he was twelve really helped me not only in the parenting arena, but in other areas as well.

After someone had made disparaging remarks to him about me, I became very upset. He said, "Well if I know the truth, and you know the truth, and Daddy knows the truth, why do you care what they think?" Ah—the wisdom of a child. He was absolutely right. His assessment of the situation not only helped me at the time, but it is a truth I've frequently returned to since then.

No matter what you do, someone will be hovering around to criticize. So when feeling vulnerable to criticism, ask, 'What is the truth here? Am I putting forth my best efforts in this area of my life or not?' If you are doing your best in a situation, why care what anyone else thinks. And if you're not, then that's something to look at. Asking and answering these questions makes you less vulnerable to the criticism of others, and leaves no reason to harbor resentment.

It's Not Personal

Take into consideration that when you think others are making snide or judgmental comments, perhaps they are not doing that at all. An innocent comment can feel like personal criticism if it strikes you in an area where you feel insecure. If you frequently feel that others are know-it-alls or that they are always one-upping you, such feelings are probably projections of your own insecurities. Healing comes through working with the feelings that are triggered in you, and allowing the truth to shine through.

The truth and the paradox is that *everything* is personal and *nothing* is personal. Everything is personal in that you react, relate and respond to other people based on how you feel about yourself. And nothing is personal because other people are doing the same thing!

The people who provoke your stuff are giving you an opportunity to look deeply at yourself. And of course, there are people who are bona fide obnoxious. Observation of obnoxious behavior (or any other kind for that matter) is not necessarily an ego projection. But if another person's behavior makes you crazy—it is. Your reactions to the behavior of other people are projections of the ego. Such projections can be healed when you become aware of and take responsibility for them, and then give them to the Spirit Within for correction. Correction is forgiveness.

The Willingness to Forgive

Forgiveness is when you give up resentment or allow room for error or weakness. The antidote for the poison of resentment is forgiveness. In your unwillingness to forgive people, you are denying them room to be mistaken, insecure or weak. We judge and attack from our own weakness, insecurity and fear, and others react in kind. This recognition fosters an increased willingness to forgive not only others, but ourselves as well.

You need not know how to forgive, you need only be willing to do so. Your willingness is an invitation to spiritual assistance. I have become better at loving and forgiving others and myself only because I have become better at asking for spiritual help. I now recognize that I cannot do it alone. Try this prayer: Dear God, I am willing to forgive (enter person's name) so that I may be free. Please help me.

Only through practicing the steps of awareness, responsibility and forgiveness can you truly come to live the law *Love one another*.

What Goes Around Comes Around

The second universal law is *What goes around comes around*. Also known as the law of giving and receiving, cause and effect, sowing and reaping, karma … Basically, all these ideas impart the same truth: You get back what you put out.

What goes around comes around is actually a fundamental law of our thought process. The acceptance of this idea offers you freedom found in knowing that you are not trapped by your circumstances. Working with this law requires willingness to make connections between your thoughts and their consequences in your life.

I found a wonderful analogy that illustrates this principle: *Your mind is like a tree, and the thoughts that enter your mind are like birds. It's not so important which birds light on a branch of your tree for a moment and then fly on. What matters is which birds you allow to build a nest in your tree and make a home there.*[12]

The thoughts that become your reality are the ones that have "nested" in your mind. Thoughts are creative energy. When we understand this, it behooves us to pay attention to the content of our thoughts.

You're probably aware of the Golden Rule: Do unto others as

you would have them do unto you. Emmet Fox took it a step further: *Think about others the way you would have them think about you.* When you think thoughts of resentment or criticism, that energy comes back to you in a multitude of ways. As you begin to embrace thoughts of love and forgiveness, that energy also comes back to you. At some level, we receive exactly what we give.

LAW THREE

༺✦༻

Do It Now Or Do It Later

At some point in our spiritual evolution, we will be healed. We will return to the remembrance that we are beings of love. We will one day, get it together. You can embark on that journey to wholeness now, or you can put if off. Growth is a requirement, not an option. You are not free to choose whether or not you will grow, but you are free to choose when.

The universe does not judge us. There are no divine beings sitting up in the sky saying, "Darn! When is she going to get it?" Instead, we attract situations and people that provide opportunities to choose whether or not to grow. Repetitive painful situations are not some kind of punishment, but are in fact, learning opportunities.

You might experience the same negative situations in job after job or relationship after relationship. In fact, you're very likely to! Negative patterns will be repeated until the pain becomes so great that you are forced to look at resolving the issue in a different way than merely getting another job or finding another mate. At that point, you may come to recognize the common denominator in every negative situation as being you. You may then come to your knees, literally or figuratively, and seek a better way.

Free will does not allow us to choose the circumstances for learning, but it does allow choice as to when we will learn the lessons set forth. The lessons are always about bringing awareness and responsibility to what's happening in our lives.

So how does the law *Do it now or do it later* apply? As you read this, you may be experiencing pain in an intimate relationship. Hypothetically, in your last relationship you were unhappy because you felt that your partner used you, invalidated you, or took you for granted and so you left the relationship. In your current relationship, everything was fine at first, but you soon began to feel used, invalidated or taken for granted. You now have two choices: You can leave the relationship and find another one, or you can choose to look more closely at what is really going on.

First, acknowledge the connection between the way you felt in your former relationship, and your current perception that your partner uses you, invalidates or takes you for granted. The empowering question becomes, 'What needs healing in me that would either attract me to situations like this, or cause me to perceive behavior that is not really there?' It doesn't matter whether they are doing it or not, it still comes down to you. You either think they are doing it when they're not, or you attracted those circumstances for a reason. You can apply this idea to any painful situation in your life.

After years of glowing reviews at her job, an acquaintance of mine received a review where she was told that she was stubborn and argumentative. Being very angry, she quit the job. A few days later, while cleaning out a drawer, she found reviews from a previous job. For years they stated that she was a great employee until the last one, which said that she was stubborn and argumentative. Faced with this information, she could have done what many do: Blame her employer. But to her credit, she sat back on her heels and thought, 'It's me!'

What led her to that drawer on that day? Whether or not you are aware of it, your Spirit is constantly guiding you toward consciousness and healing. The first step is awareness, *"Oh My God. It's Me!"* And then, responsibility: Ask and answer the question: 'Do I want to work with this now, or do I want to play it out a few more times until the pain is greater?' Eventually the inner work will have to be done. *Do it now or do it later.* The choice is yours.

It Can Be Hard To "Do It Now"

Sometimes things come up in our lives that we really don't want to deal with right now. One of my relatives once jokingly said, "Sheryl, if we don't deal with the conflict in our relationship now, we'll have to deal with it in another life."

"Fine," I replied. "I'll deal with in the next lifetime because I don't want to deal with it now." A year or two later, through my spiritual inner work, the relationship was healed. But that came about only after I recognized that my resentment toward her was only hurting me.

You come to really understand the concept of *Do it now or do it later* when you realize that what you are doing or thinking *now* is hurting you. How are you feeling now? What are you thinking now? Here again, practice forgiveness, not condemnation. If you don't know how to forgive, ask for Divine help: 'Dear God, help me do what I cannot do for myself.'

LAW FOUR

There's No Free Lunch!

Believe it or not "free lunch" shows up in the dictionary, "something given with no expectation of responsibility." As children, most of us had our basic needs met without expectation of responsibility. Once we become adults, however, it came as a rude awakening to realize that little is given without expectations.

One of my son's friends said, "The problem with my generation is that we want money without work, knowledge without study and spirituality without sacrifice. It's going to come back and bite us in the butt." His statement contains truth that harkens to the idea that something of value doesn't come from nothing.

We mostly think of a free lunch in terms of economics. But then, who wouldn't want a free lunch in the form of winning or inheriting money? It's a fantasy I sometimes indulge in too! We've heard the stories about people acquiring an excess of money through inheritance, lawsuits, the lottery or whatever, and within a few years they exist in the same state of lack as before they got it.

I know of a woman who won the lottery. She says that it is the worst thing that happened. Relatives and friends came out of the woodwork asking for money. And her marriage was on the rocks because she and her husband had different views on how to spend the winnings. She wishes she had never won. Nothing comes without a cost. This is not to say that one could not attain an excess of money and enjoy it, share it and use it wisely. Still, there is no free lunch in that it will take inner work to be able to do that.

Of course we gain knowledge through study, but the greatest knowledge comes through experience. While we may have some experience with there being no free lunch, most of us have little experience with God's grace. God's will for us is not struggle, frustration and feeling that life is hard and unfair. God gives us grace, love, abundance and eternal blessings—without expectations. And while God doesn't demand a price, there is one. We receive God's blessings as we *give* them to others, and thus come home to the truth that giving and receiving are the same.

How does forgiveness fit into there being no free lunch? The Bible says that whatever you ask for in prayer, believe that it is granted you, and you will get it. All too many people think that prayer promises something for nothing. However, it goes on to say that whenever you pray, if you hold anything against another forgive it—let it go so that God may also forgive you.[13]

In truth, God does not forgive because God does not condemn. Nevertheless, God is the Source of forgiveness that enables forgiveness of self and others. God's gifts are freely given, but when we hold onto resentment, fear and guilt, we separate from the Source of all good, and are thus unable to receive all that is so valuable and available.

When Nothing Seems to Help …

Do you ever have those days when you feel that all your efforts are fruitless? Over twenty years ago when I was building my business, I had one of those days. I laugh now, but on that day I actually considered going home to have a good cry. Immersed in self pity, I glanced up at a motivational calendar on my desk and read the following:

> *When nothing seems to help,*
> *I go and watch the stonecutter,*
> *hammering away at his rock*
> *perhaps a hundred times without*
> * as much as a crack showing in it.*
> *Yet at the hundred and first blow*
> *it splits in two, and I know that it*
> *was not that blow that did it,*
> *but all that had gone before.[14]*

I read it again, and again. I got it! I realized that everything was okay exactly as it was. I arose from my desk and went forth to have a happy and productive day.

I love this poem more than any other. I have embraced its

message many times over the years. The stonecutter reminds us that life is a process. Everything we do, every thought we think, plants seeds for tomorrow's fruit. When we water those seeds with a mixture of hope and love—life becomes juicy and ripe with purpose, creativity and joy.

Spiritual Practice

As you diligently practice spiritual principles it will often seem as if nothing is happening! You won't necessarily be healed tomorrow, next year or a decade from now. Healing is a process and a practice. You'll slowly begin to recognize that you are handling your problems differently; you feel tranquil more often, and you even seem to like yourself more. You may have moments of great sadness and moments of incredible joy. Most profoundly, you begin to recognize that everything seems to be working perfectly for your good and the good of all concerned.

The spiritual principles you choose to practice are the tools that get your mind, and thus your life back on track. A helpful analogy to spiritual practice is the exit ramps on a freeway. While on the freeway if you take the wrong exit, you're okay because you know where the freeway is—you need only return to it to continue your journey. Spiritual principles work the same way. Even with much practice, you will still fall into darkness or despair, but you now have the tools to bring you back to the truth. The truth is that God is always with you.

Be aware, however, that at some point in your spiritual practice you might begin to wonder if ignorance is bliss after all. Once you have brought a certain amount of awareness and responsibility to your life, you may begin to beat yourself up over the negative stuff you continually create. When I indulge in my negative patterns even though I know that I am blocking the flow of love, creativity and abundance, I sometimes choose not to stop what

I'm doing in the moment. But at least I know that what I am doing has consequences. When I did not comprehend that I was creating the negative experiences in my life, I was far from blissful! There is no bliss in ignorance.

Bringing It All Together

This chapter has set in place three steps to growth and healing: Awareness, responsibility and forgiveness. They are clarified with the application to four spiritual laws. Were there any growth steps or laws that you felt strong resistance about? Those are probably the ones you need to work with the most. Spiritual practice is cumulative, one practice building on the next. Life becomes your classroom when you experiment with the application of these growth steps and spiritual laws. It is one thing to intellectually know spiritual principles, but it is quite another to experience their effects. Take one law each week or even each month, and ask the Inner Presence to help you experience the truth of it. And then pay attention to where your life is leading you.

As you act in accordance with spiritual laws, you become happier, more peaceful, and move on to living a life filled with purpose. It is also important to realize that although you can do nothing by yourself, you can do anything when you join with the strength of God, which is only a prayer away.

And so, as you go about your life, heed this comment by Woody Allen: *"Eighty percent of success is showing up."* You show up for your life when you bring awareness and responsibility to how you are living it.

IS GOD REAL?

"Sometimes I think God is real. But other times I think God is just a fantasy human beings came up with to make themselves feel better."

"Do you pray or meditate?" I asked.

"No."

"Well if you do so, you'll come to know for yourself whether or not God is real."

I engaged in this conversation with someone while writing this chapter on prayer. Reading or hearing the words "God is real" will mean nothing to you without personal experience. God is not your enemy, but a most intimate and beloved Friend. You will come to know this truth when you establish a relationship with this Presence through prayer and meditation. Because each practice is so important, I have dedicated this chapter to prayer and the following one to meditation.

I used to wonder how prayer could help anything. Once I started doing it, I found out. You will find prayers throughout this book. Some will resonate with you more than others. Use them. Memorize the ones that speak to you. When you memorize a prayer it becomes handy and available in your mind. The healing power of prayer cannot be experienced unless you pray.

One may wonder just who or what they're supposed to pray to: God, Jesus, Holy Spirit, Inner Presence ... I don't think that the force of Love in this universe cares what we call it. We could pray to: "To Whom It May Concern" with the same effect. Prayer changes us. With prayer, we acknowledge that there is a power greater than ourselves—one of love, wisdom, peace and strength.

"When Do I Pray?"

You may know the line from the Bible, *pray without ceasing*. Obviously, few of us could pray every waking moment. We may get tripped up in thinking that we must set aside time for prayer. To pray without ceasing means to pray anytime—anywhere. To pray without ceasing is to recognize that God is with you wherever you go. Through your prayers you invite God's presence into your consciousness.

You can pray when you wake up, in the shower, in the car, when you're exercising or doing a task; and when you're with family, friends or clients. The idea is to recognize that you need the Source of light and love present throughout your day.

Prayer is particularly miraculous in areas of temptation. Whether you are tempted to be angry, impatient, feel sorry for yourself, or whatever, the answer is—pray! Learning to pray all the time is a process. Start with moments—take an area in your life where you struggle or feel frustration. Let's say that it's overeating. Bring awareness to the time of day when you are most likely to indulge, and pray first. Pray for God's strength and grace before entering the kitchen, you'll have more control. I admit that frequently I don't remember to do this and sometimes, don't even want to! But when I do it, the results are better. Be alert to your areas of temptation and pray first.

Peace Is a Prayer Away

One of the first areas I applied prayer to was anger. Whenever I am not at peace, I pray. Initially in my spiritual practice there was a particular prayer from *A Course in Miracles* that stood out for me, and although I had memorized it, I had not experienced its power.

One morning while driving to work, I churned over what someone had done to me. I remembered the prayer and repeated it in my mind. Several hours later, I realized that I had not thought about that person for hours, and that I was at peace about the situation. After that experience this particular prayer became a mainstay in my spiritual practice.

Whenever you feel angry, guilty, fearful or down-and-out, as sincerely as you can, say the following prayer:

I must have decided wrongly, because I am not at peace.
I made this decision myself, and I can also decide otherwise.
I want to decide otherwise, because I want to be at peace.
I do not feel guilty, because the Holy Spirit will undo all the
consequences of my wrong decision if I will let Him.
I choose to let Him, by allowing Him to decide for God, for me.[15]

I used to need that prayer several times a day! It never ceases to amaze me how this simple prayer brings me to peace. For years I did not know why it was so effective. I now understand that in praying such a prayer, you are aware that you are not at peace (this is big, in and of itself), and you are at least willing to choose peace. If you weren't, you wouldn't bother saying a prayer in the first place. With prayer, you make another choice. You invite God's healing presence into your mind and heart, and thus come home to peace.

"What Do I Pray?"

One night a friend called to tell me that her husband had been diagnosed with a life-threatening illness. She asked me to pray for him. Even though I had been praying for years, I got off the phone and thought, 'What do I pray?' Have you felt that way too?

Sometimes we put off prayer because we feel that our prayers have to be wordy and profound. Not at all. Mostly I simply think of the person and envision him or her surrounded by God's healing presence. I also have pet prayers that I use in particular situations. You'll find many of them throughout this book. Over the years I've also picked up prayers from many sources. A favorite is Marianne Williamson's book, *Illuminata*, which contains prayers for many situations.

You can also take favorite passages from the Bible or any book that inspires you and make them into prayers: 'Dear God, today, please help me meet myself and others totally without judgment so that I may experience tremendous release and deep peace.'[16] Above all, please know that it is just as effective to call out to a Higher Presence with whatever words stir your heart.

Does God Help Those Who Help Themselves?

In *Adventures in Prayer*, Catherine Marshall wrote:

> *"I believe the old cliché, 'God helps those who help themselves,' is not only misleading but often dead wrong. My most spectacular answers to prayers have come when I was so helpless, so out of control as to be able to do nothing at all for myself."*

But she *did* help herself. She prayed. "My most spectacular answers to prayers … " When we cry any version of "Help!" God answers, *Here I am! Behold! I stand at the door and knock; if anyone hears my voice and opens the door I will come in.*[17] This verse tells us much about how God operates. Let's look at it more closely.

Here I am! Behold! I stand at the door; God is present and available within our mind and heart.

And knock; we have been endowed with free will, thus God will not break the door down but instead, awaits our welcome.

If anyone hears my voice; within our very helplessness, we may be receptive to the Inner Voice, or we may not. Sometimes we are so caught up in our powerless state of mind that the only voice we hear is that of our own fear. But each one of us has a limit to how much pain we can handle. Once reached, on some level we cry, "Enough already! I can't help myself!"

And opens the door; in our very recognition that we need God, we hear the Voice, and are then willing to surrender our mind and heart to this loving presence.

I will come in; and then, God is here, within and around us. We know this.

In crisis, we acknowledge the knock; hear the Inner Voice and open the door to healing. But then, a few days, weeks or months later the crisis is over and we proceed to slam the door. Most of us begin our relationship with God this way. In time, however, we realize that if God can be trusted in an emergency, how much more could this Presence offer us if we just propped the door open permanently? The Source of all light and love has endowed you with free will and will not force itself upon you. Through your prayers you say, "Yes! Come unto me."

Cause or Effect?

Most of us have had the experience of thinking that our prayers were not answered, if even heard. This is because we often pray on the level of effect rather than the level of cause. The law of cause and effect is the most fundamental law there is. God cannot intervene between our thoughts and their results. In other words, God does not fix the outer conditions in our lives. But what God does do, is heal the thoughts (cause) that brought about the outer condition (effect) in the first place.

Let's say that you are fearful about a condition or circumstance, and so you pray to God to fix it thinking that the fear will be removed as well. Even if God did fix the outer conditions, it would only be temporary if the cause of that effect were not brought to the light.

The basic conflict we have is between love and fear. God cannot magically remove fear from our minds, but we can bring God to our fearful thoughts for healing. Prayer on the level of effect: 'Dear God, please take away my fear. Fix this or do that.' Prayer on the level of cause: 'Dear God, heal me. Heal my perceptions. Help me see this situation through your eyes of love rather than my eyes of fear.' Even if this were the only prayer you ever prayed, you would experience much healing because you will have sought and found the cause. Prayers prayed on the causal level are the means to healing.

When you go to God in prayer, forget the things you think you need or want. You have but one need, and that is a healed mind. Fear stems from a sense of separation from God. A healed mind is one that is joined with God. In truth, you have already been given everything. God is all abundance, love, wisdom and strength. As a creation of God, so too, are you.

Praying For Others
Through prayer you become a channel through which God extends love into the world. So many people touch our lives not only in our immediate vicinity, but also in the world at large. It would be impossible to pray for them all. I used to feel guilty when I'd forget to pray for certain people. You cannot be all things to all people, even in prayer. So for whom do you pray? Who are you thinking about? Who do you feel inspired to pray for? Who is standing in front of you in person or in your mind?

When praying for others, keep in mind that the purpose of prayer is not to fix other people or their lives. You may pray for a person to be cured of an illness because you don't want to lose him or see her suffer; however, you do not know the plan for that person's spiritual evolution. You might pray for a change to occur in someone's life when in fact, that person may need those experiences in order to live the life they are meant to live. Even though suffering is not part of God's plan for us, going through it can bring us to a higher level of service, compassion and understanding of others and ourselves. Your prayers need not be complicated: 'Dear God, I acknowledge that he is enfolded in your love.'

Let Go And Let God
When I met my husband I became a full time parent to his nine-year-old son. And yes, that was a pregnancy all right! Being a parent is one of the hardest things that I have done. It is probably the area in my life where I have learned the most about the tremendous healing power of prayer. I don't know how a parent gets through child rearing without it.

Our son's teenage years were especially trying for us as I imagine they are for most people. It would be impossible to recount the many miracles prayer has brought to my family. When I reflect on the many times I prayed for my son, my husband and myself, in retrospect I see that the most effectual prayers were those of surrender.

Our son had problems with school. It seemed that we had done everything possible to help him, but nothing worked for very long. One day in total despair, I sat in my car in front of his school and prayed, 'Dear God, I don't know what to do. I can't take it anymore. You take it. I surrender our lives to you.' Immediately I heard, 'Sheryl, you are a perfect child of God, and so is your son. Just as God works in your life, God is also working in his.' I felt so released. Lo and behold, the very next day we found a new school or actually, it found us. I believe this occurrence may have changed his life in ways we will probably never even be aware of.

Although the new school was a turning point, our beloved

child being who he is, continued to give me multiple opportunities to learn more about the power of prayer. With each new trial, I'd first try to figure out how to fix the problem but would soon remember, 'Oh yeah, pray!' As I surrendered my fears and worries about him to God, I came to the knowledge based on experience that God could take better care of him than we could. Instead of my prayers being, 'Dear God, fix him, *please*! And fix him this week!' they became, 'Help me see him as a perfect, whole being. Help me be the mother that You want me to be for him.'

The important point is that I learned to not pray fix-it prayers, but let-go-and-let-God prayers. Why is this so important? Again, we come to cause and effect. Fix-it prayers remain at the level of effect. They don't resolve our anxiety or fix whatever it is we are attempting to fix. When you let go and let God be God, you surrender your fear to be at one with the Source of all guidance, strength and love. When I surrendered my fear, then and only then did I hear God's guidance, which then led to divine solutions.

My son has been one of my greatest spiritual teachers. Loving him and raising him taught me time and time again to let go and let God. Through my willingness to do so, I have seen the miraculous power of prayer at work in all areas of our lives. You will too.

Prayers of the Ego

Watch out for the ego when praying for others. An acquaintance related to me that she had a problem with her daughter's lifestyle. She had prayed to God to put a crown of thorns on her daughter's head until she changed her ways. She said that she thought the prayer had worked because her daughter's life had been miserable for the past two years. I was appalled! I asked her if she really thought of God as a god of vengeance. "Absolutely! Absolutely, God is a god of vengeance," she replied vehemently.

One day as I thought about that conversation, I opened *A*

Course in Miracles to this: *They call upon a vengeful god, and it is he who seems to answer them. Hell cannot be asked for another, and then escaped by those who ask for it.*[18]

Hell is not a place we might go when we die, but is instead, a state of mind. When we judge and condemn others, we keep ourselves in hell. Have you noticed? The most healing prayer is, 'Dear God, heal my mind. Heal my perceptions. Help me see this person with your loving vision.'

We Need One Another

Our prayers are often answered through other people. The following story provides a great example of this:

A big flood was coming and a man stood at the front window of his house and prayed to God to save him. As the water began to rise, a woman came by in a rowboat and yelled, "Come on in buddy! Get in the boat so you don't drown." The man replied, "No, I prayed to God to save me. I'll be fine."

As the water continued to rise, the man was forced up to the second story of his house, and a big boat came by. Someone yelled, "Get in the boat, I'll save you!" The man again replied, "No, I prayed to God to save me. I'll be fine."

As the water continued to rise, the man escaped to the roof of his house, and a helicopter came by. The pilot yelled, "Hey man, grab this rope, I'll save you." The man said, "No, I prayed to God to save me. I'll be fine." He drowned.

He ascended to Heaven and said to God, "I don't understand it! I've been your faithful servant all these years. I think about you day and night. I prayed for you to save me. Why did I drown?" God replied, "I don't understand it either. I sent you two boats and a helicopter!"

The man had three people come by to save him. What was he looking for? What miracle was he expecting God to do? Instead of recognizing our need for one another, we frequently separate ourselves from others. One of the ways God is present on this planet is through you. When you feel lost in darkness and long to see the light, look to the person in front of you—as you see the light in another, it is a reflection of your own.

"But I Don't Believe in God!"
No problem. Pray.

> *God,*
> *I don't know who you are.*
> *I don't know what you are.*
> *I don't know if I trust you.*
> *I don't even know if I believe in you.*
> *But in this moment,*
> *in this situation,*
> *I am willing to **pretend***
> *that you are real.*
> *I am willing to **pretend***
> *that I have total trust in you.*
> *In this moment,*
> *I am willing to **pretend***
> *that you are my Friend.*

And so, as you go about your life, "act as if." Through your willingness to pretend that God is real, you will come to know without a doubt that God is—*real.*

YOU DO NOT WALK ALONE

For the first thirty years of my life, I rarely thought about God. Had I been asked if I believed in God, I suppose I would have said yes, perhaps being afraid to say no. But through prayer and meditation I made the most amazing discovery—God is real! God is alive and well in this universe! God is within you and me—right here, right now! Wow!

If you want to discover this too, then a consistent practice of prayer and meditation is the most important thing you could devote yourself to. In time, you will come to see the presence of God in your life as clearly as you see your hand. Both prayer and meditation are essential if you desire to grow spiritually. The previous chapter on prayer is the perfect predecessor for us to talk about meditation.

Meditation Disciplines Your Mind

The most important reason to meditate is that it introduces you to the still small Voice within. On a practical level, meditation trains your mind. Meditation is difficult for the undisciplined mind, yet it is through the practice that you learn to discipline your mind. Once you begin to meditate, you will probably be surprised to find that your mind wanders a lot! Meditation brings to your awareness just how undisciplined your mind really is, hence the need for mind training.

We want to be happy, we want inner peace, but we cannot enter such states while our minds are undisciplined. If your life is chaotic it's because your mind is chaotic. You can return chaos to harmony with a disciplined mind. Discipline is meant to develop a state of order and obedience by training and control. Training means to develop or form habits, thoughts or behavior using discipline. Your thoughts create your life. If you have no control over your thoughts—well then, there you go. You cannot change your life if you have no control over your thoughts. Mind training is not easy. But don't fall into thinking that you are a failure at meditation because you can't seem to do it. Initially, meditation is difficult for everyone.

There are many ways to meditate. There isn't a right way to do it. Once you decide that you want to meditate, it is likely that you will be guided to a discipline that will be most helpful to you. Essentially, the practice involves bringing your mind to a single focus, whether it is to words, an object or your breath.

Let's say that you have chosen to meditate on the phrase, "Peace to my mind my thoughts are still." Meditation practice may go something like this: 'Peace to my mind my thoughts are still—Darn! I have to pay that bill tomorrow! Okay, okay—peace to my mind my thoughts are—I just can't believe what my son did this morning! How could—okay, okay, peace to my mind my thoughts are still, peace to my—I'm so fat, I need to start a diet, I need—okay, get off that—peace to my mind …'

This is very normal. Simply bring awareness to the thoughts that come up, and then gently push them aside. Return to your point of focus. Some days, you just won't be able to quiet your mind. This is okay. Meditation is a nurturing time, not a time to beat yourself up.

Exercise is a great analogy to the practice of meditation. When you exercise and meditate consistently, you achieve better results than someone who doesn't. Just as you don't become great at exercising, you probably won't become great at meditating either. Meditation is a practice.

Guided meditation tapes can be extremely helpful, and some-times life changing. Such tapes come in all varieties, from medita-tions designed for relaxation to those that focus on various behavior and thought patterns. Guided meditations can be instrumental in enabling you to become aware of and thus break through inner blocks and negative patterns.

Practical Aspects of Meditation

How much time does it take? That's up to you. Many people make the mistake of attempting to sit down to meditate for twenty or thirty minutes the first time they try it. This is like trying to run a mile when you've never even walked around the block. A good way to begin the practice is to spend a few minutes sitting quietly and alone each day, without trying to do anything. This won't be as easy as it sounds. Once you can do this, you can then move into focusing your mind. Begin your daily practice with one-minute exercises. As you progress, longer periods of time come more easily to you. It is important to understand that duration is not the point, entering the silence is.

And then there are those who meditate on a mountaintop for hours or days at a time. Most of us are not on that path. I've read about people who have spent years in monasteries or spiritual retreats, yet once they returned to the world, they were just as crazed as the rest of us! Learn to bring your spiritual practice into your daily life. When you become crazed in this world, turning inward with meditation will help you approach your circum-stances with a lot less fear.

Along with the mountaintop experience, forget the lotus position. Most of us cannot sit in the lotus position more that five minutes without knee pain. Initially it will be hard enough to focus thought in one place, let alone trying to contend with bodily pain. Get into a comfortable position. Meditation is easier and more effective in a sitting position, although as your mind becomes more disciplined you may find that you can also meditate while lying down, walking or while practicing an art or hobby.

When is the best time to meditate? That's up to you. Through practice you learn to come to it when you need it. Nevertheless, meditating in the morning can serve to set a more peaceful tone for your day. But if your kids are jumping up and down on your bed when you wake up, obviously this is not a good time to meditate. As soon as you can, take a few minutes. When your mind becomes disciplined, you will be able to meditate anywhere. Once before an anxiety producing event, I actually meditated in a public restroom! Before sleep is also a beneficial time. Even an instant of communing with God, being thankful for the day and its gifts will make a difference.

It is up to you to decide how much time and effort you are willing to give to meditation, prayer and the practice of living your spiritual principles. The time and effort should not be thought of as a nuisance, but as something that will enhance your life.

What about Fear?
Sometimes while in meditation, you might feel uncomfortable, anxious or fearful. When this occurs, if possible remain still for one or two more minutes. Often you will get past the discomfort. If not, simply stop. Why would one experience fear or anxiety while in meditation? Meditation calls to our attention the fear-filled and anxious content of our thoughts. The ego doesn't want you to be aware of what you're thinking which is why it vehemently resists meditation. Have you noticed? The practice teaches you to recognize the ego (fear), if only for a moment, and also enables you to release your fear and return to peace. Before every meditation ask the Inner Presence to be with you.

Nothing Is Supposed To Happen

Many people think that something is supposed to happen in meditation. Nothing is supposed to happen. Meditation simply brings you to an awareness of the present moment. I've been meditating for years and could count on one hand the life changing experiences that occurred while in meditation. And I'll add here that those experiences were always spontaneous and surprising. You cannot force spiritual growth and healing. Strain will not bring you closer to God. Such effort will only preclude the experience of God.

In meditation you want to rest in the silence. It's not a time to beat up on yourself: 'I can't do this. I'm a failure. I can't stay on a diet. I can't find a job I like. I can't even find a man I like. And *now*, I can't even meditate!' Sound familiar? Expecting immediate results from meditation would be like expecting to play Beethoven's Moonlight Sonata after one piano lesson. When you think about it, wouldn't it be ridiculous to give up something because you weren't great at it the first few times you tried it? Yet this is often what we do with meditation. Above all else, meditation requires patience, practice and perseverance.

"I'm Too Stressed Out!"

"My life is a mess! I'm stressed out! I just can't meditate!" When you think that you are too stressed out to meditate—this is precisely when you need it the most. It's during these difficult times that you most need to enter the silence, and when you can most dramatically experience the effects of it.

At first you may meditate for 20 minutes, but then spend another 23 1/2 hours feeling stressed, angry or fearful. Your willingness to even attempt to meditate, if only for a moment, indicates that you are ready, at least on some level, to experience peace. These moments of peace begin to string together like a strand of graduated pearls, one building on the next. And soon, peace begins to permeate your mind. Through practice, you will come to realize that you do have control of your thoughts, perceptions, emotions, and your very destiny.

The Fruits of Meditation

Meditation must be practiced, not merely read about. Meditation is a tool that enables you to live more consciously and more joyfully. The benefits of meditation are countless. Through meditation you can gain guidance on all areas of your life. You may not hear an answer to a problem while in meditation, but one often shows up later in a book, conversation or whatever. The "right" answer to a problem is one that carries with it a sense of peace.

When I meditate for a few minutes before a phone call or an encounter with someone, it helps to bring about a more peaceful interaction. I don't always remember to do this before an encounter, but when I handle it badly, you can bet I remember afterward!

It is also important to pay attention to what comes up in your meditations. Perhaps a person will pop into your mind. Call them; send a note or a silent blessing of love. Or you might receive an idea regarding something you have been thinking about or working on. Act on the messages you receive in meditation.

A great benefit of meditation that I have experienced is that I have become more intuitive and even somewhat psychic. No, I don't see the future, but as a doctor, my diagnostic skills have been greatly enhanced. I can intuitively tune into what is going on with a patient, beyond their physical pain. Since your intuition is the Voice of Spirit communicating with you, an increased ability to hear that Voice is a great gift and should not be underestimated. With this strengthened ability, you are able to gain guidance in all aspects of your life.

"Help!"

Not long after I began to meditate, I went through a major healing period in my life. While in the throes of it, one afternoon I sat on my porch and sobbed, "Help Me!" Immediately I felt a weight, a hand if you will, gently push my head down taking me deep inside my Self.

While I do recall some of what I heard there, the most important thing is that an hour later as I lifted my head, I felt the most profound state of peace. I knew without a doubt that these words from *A Course in Miracles* were true: *You do not walk alone. God's angels hover near and all about. God's love surrounds you. And of this you can be sure—God will never leave you comfortless.*[19]

"Thank You"

Not long after this experience, as I sat down to meditate one morning the words, *Thank You, Thank You, Thank You* arose spontaneously from my innermost being. I felt such profound gratitude for the peace that had begun to encompass my mind.

Throughout this book, I have written about the healing that prayer and meditation have brought to my life. That is why I wrote this book. And while I am far from being a healed and perfect being, the practice has carried me to a place of enjoyment and appreciation for each day of my life. Reading my words, however, will not bring you to this place. Prayer and meditation will.

And so, as you go about your life, meditate on the following God inspired invitation:

Come to me.
Know me.
Seek me
where I can be found,
within.

I am in your heart.
I am in your mind.
You do not walk alone.
Lift your mind
beyond this world,
and come home
to me.
Rest with me
in the silence of your heart.
I am your guidance.
I am your strength.
I am your love.
Come to me.
Know me.
Rest with me
and be
at peace.

4 TRUTH IN STORY

Through stories we recognize the
commonality of our journeys,
and that we are not alone
but connected
through the experiences we have.

– Darlene Montgomery,
Conscious Women Conscious Lives

―――――――――――――――――

Please God,
Enlarge my heart with a story,
and change me by the characters
I meet there.

– Ken Gire, Windows of the Soul

LOST, AND FOUND

Haunted by the memory
Of home
I become still.
From the silence
A Voice beckons

To the stranger
I am now.
Lost, astray and
Homeless,
Inheritance gone,

I long to return
And stranger
Be no more
In the land
That is
My home.

From the silence,
Still,
A Voice beckons:
Home waits. Hasten,
For you are not lost
But found.[20]

Leaving Home

Give heed to the story of a father and his two sons.[21] One day the youngest son comes to his father and asks for his inheritance. He wants to go off on his own and make his way in the world. I can so relate to the young son, albeit, without the inheritance. I was one of those kids who couldn't wait to be adult. I even came out of the womb feet first! From day one I questioned authority, I wanted my own identity, I wanted to rewrite the rules, I wanted to fail or succeed on my own—in short, I wanted my own life. Whether or not you were as independent and rebellious as I, you can probably still relate to the desire to leave the family nest.

In the story, the young man's father didn't try to talk him out of leaving home, just like most of our parents didn't discourage it. Leaving home is integral to the process of growing up. When the son asked for his inheritance, his father simply gave him what he asked for.

On another level, the universe always gives us what we ask for, no more, no less. If you want to know what you have asked for, look no further than your very life. Your life experiences reveal what you have asked for, and what you have been willing to have. When you let your life teach you what you *really* want, your experiences become a gift.

Let us now be a fly on the wall and glean lessons from what the two sons learn from their experiences.

The Far Country

The young son takes what is his and goes forth to the far country. The far country is not a place but a state of mind. The journey to the far county is one we all take because it is not so much about the desire to leave the family home as it represents a state of consciousness—one of being separate from our Source. The trek to the far country is a detour from the Truth that God is an active and present partner in our lives. You might think that you haven't separated from God if you didn't stray from religion, but do you know God as a living and ever present Source of guidance, love, abundance and strength? Most of us don't know this on an experiential level.

The very fact that you are on this earth indicates that you have traveled to the far country. This world is a place of fear, lack and limitation—it is not our true home. And on some level, each one of us knows that this is true. The memory of home haunts us, calling for our return.

We travel far from the womb of God's love, but eventually we will take another journey—the journey home. Looking for home outside of us is futile because that's not where it is. The homeward journey is a return to the remembrance that love is our home, and that home is within.

A Lost and Prodigal Son

While in the far country, the young son spends all his money having a good time. After squandering his inheritance, he soon finds himself impoverished and in need. To add to his misery a famine has taken over the land. In desperation he hires himself out to a farmer who gives him the task of feeding pigs. Lost and hungry, he is tempted to eat the food he feeds the pigs, for no one gives him anything.

The son has hit rock bottom. Once he was a wealthy man but is now starving and feeding pigs. He left home to find freedom, but instead found lack and limitation. He became more enslaved than ever before.

One night he sadly contemplates his life and cries: "I am lost and astray. And I am homeless—a stranger in a strange land. I have wasted my inheritance in exchange for nothing of value. Woe is me! Oh how I long to return and stranger be no more in the land that is my home!"

A Turning Point

The story doesn't tell us how many years he spent in the far country before he came to despair. Perhaps he was experiencing a midlife crisis—a turning point that often leads to higher choices. Whether at midlife or not, most of us reach a point when we cry, "Enough! Uncle! There must be a better way to live my life than this!"

Having reached such a turning point, he experienced an "Aha!" moment: "My father's servants have more to eat than I do." It is interesting that it wasn't a guilty conscience that sent him home, but hunger. Hunger, an appetite that must regularly be satisfied in order to sustain life. Yet beyond our striving lies a hunger for that place which will truly sustain life—the home of God's love.

Hungry for food and home the son thinks, "I will arise and return to my father." The memory of home is implanted within us. We can deny it or push it away, but we cannot forget because we indeed always hunger for home. We may have vague persistent feelings, "I'm different from everybody else; I don't belong here; something is missing." Or it might be expressed in the anxiety we feel—or in those panic attacks or insomnia. Maybe it's expressed in the way we walk the world in worry, anger and fear. Such states of mind tell us that we are not at home in this world. A turning point occurs when you are willing to tune out the song of the worldly sirens and listen instead to the gentle and poignant Inner Voice that beckons: "Arise! Home awaits you. Hasten there."

We are not asked to leave this world, but rather to arise in consciousness and find home within it. Our true inheritance is not money or things; it is the remembrance that God is the source of all good. Once we remember this—instead of living in a place of isolation and fear, our lives become filled with purpose and meaning.

Lack and Limitation

We have separated from the consciousness of God as our source of abundance and have instead fallen into a consciousness of lack and limitation. No matter how many blessings embrace our lives, we still feel that there is not enough or that something is missing. Stories abound of people who have won or inherited millions, and yet a few years later find themselves impoverished and in need. Financial wealth does not heal an underlying consciousness of lack and limitation. Keep in mind that a scarcity consciousness is not only about money. We may experience lack in health, loving relationships or in creative fulfillment. When the son thought, "I will arise and go home to my father," he looked away from his apparent lack and limitation. God is not a presence of lack because lack is only a state of mind—it is not reality.

As you traverse through the far country there is a Guide within who reminds you that home is here now; and who reminds you that you cannot be separate from your Source any more than a wave can be separate from the ocean. Home is the awareness, understanding and knowledge that you are a creation of God and are therefore abundant in every facet of life. This is your true inheritance. Your true inheritance is available right now—awaiting only your recognition of it.

God Meets You Where You Are

The son sets off for home. While still a long way off his father sees him and runs to him, he embraces and kisses him fervently. It was as if his father had been looking for him since he left. And so it is. God does not turn away from us, we turn away from God. With even the slightest willingness to turn in a new direction, God meets us where we are.

Inheritance Restored

On the journey home the son prepares a confession: "Father, I have sinned against you and God. I am no longer worthy to be called your son." The father, however, not only interrupts him, he totally ignores the confession of sin and unworthiness. Instead, he calls to his servants and says, "Bring out the best robe and put it on him. Put a ring on his finger, shoes on his feet, and kill the fatted calf. Let's have a feast and celebrate!"

The Bible speaks of the "robe of righteousness."[22] Righteousness means right relationship with God; the ring symbolizes union and the shoes symbolize freedom. Upon bestowing these gifts upon his child, he restored him to his true inheritance: You are my blessed and beloved child in whom I am well pleased.

If we were to get a worldly inheritance of money or possessions, it could quickly and easily be used up. But our true inheritance can never be used up because it is within us. The Source of all abundance, love, wisdom and strength is inexhaustible. Once we know this, all good is available right now. But while unaware of this truth, we remain in a consciousness of lack and limitation.

Self-Condemnation

The young son came home in survival mode: "I am no longer worthy to be called your son. I will survive as one of your servants!" He was not expecting unconditional love, grace and abundance, but punishment. We too feel that we have done wrong and fear punishment, and thus we project those feelings onto a wrathful and punishing god, but that's not who or what God is. God does not punish but instead, calls us to return.

We all fall into doubt, fear and self-condemnation—daily! But the father had no desire to address his child's condemnation. It's not God who says that you are wretched and miserable—you tell yourself that.

The father didn't need to say, "I forgive you," because he had never condemned his child. We condemn ourselves and then project those feelings onto a god that we think will condemn us too. Sadly, some people never escape feeling like sinners. In their own condemnation they are far away from home—they have traveled far to set up house in a distant country, and are perhaps, filled with despair.

You must come to understand here and now that God does not judge, condemn or seek to punish you. God is love. We harbor a strange desire to cling to our perceived mistakes and failures, but God absolves them all. Do you honestly believe that God, who loves you unconditionally, is going to say, "You wretched, miserable sinner! Give me back that robe!" Would the God that is revealed in this story do that? No!

We all feel that we have fallen short of God's will. We all feel on some level that we are unworthy and that we are sinners. It's not God who judges us as sinners—we do that to ourselves. God sees us as we are in Truth: Sinless, blameless and valuable. The father immediately interrupted his son when he claimed sin, blame and unworthiness, and instead restored him to the full remembrance that his children are his treasure. You, too, are God's treasure. Now is the time to leave a god of fear and return to the God of Love.

Be Still an Instant

It's not that we depart to the far country in one giant step—we run there every single day. *A Course in Miracles* has a lesson that begins with: *I will be still an instant and go home.*" [23] The first time I lectured on this story, I woke up in an angry mood! Many times throughout the day I felt guided to meditate on, I will be still an instant and go home. By that evening I came to the realization that we leave home again and again every day.

We leave home when we are angry and resentful. We leave

home in our worry and anxiety. We leave home when we feel sorry for ourselves. We leave home when we let the world and other people define who we are. In a multitude of ways—every single day, we leave the home of Love and enter a world of fear. Most of us have not yet returned. But as I discovered that day, in any moment, we can be still an instant and enfold ourselves in God's loving embrace.

Another Lost and Prodigal Son

Here we meet the older son who has just as much to teach us as the younger one. He, too, is a lost and prodigal son. Let's look at why.

When the older son returns from the field he hears the sounds of a celebration. He calls to one of the servants and asks, "What's going on?" The servant replies, "Your brother has come home." Hearing this, the older son is filled with anger, "That's not fair!"

In many families there is usually at least one person who in some way resorts to, "Mom loved him best!" Or "She got more than I did!" Or "That's not fair!" You might not be the family member who does this, but perhaps you look out into the world and compare yourself with other people, "They get more than me! It's not fair!"

The older son refuses to enter the festivities. When his father speaks to him the son says, "I've never disobeyed you. I've stayed here all these years. I've done everything you've asked, but you have never given me a feast!"

The father replies, "I love you. Everything I have is yours and has always been yours. You are forever at home with me, but your brother was lost and now he's found." Here again, God meets you where you are. This ends the story of the lost and prodigal son as it is told in the Bible. Nevertheless, it has much more to teach us.

We return to the older son who seemingly hasn't left home. He lived in the midst of plenty, but yet had no apparent consciousness of his father's love for him. If he did, wouldn't he too have rejoiced when his brother came home? But no! His brother came home and he was angry.

By all appearances the older son did everything right. Inside, however, he was filled with bitterness and resentment. He felt contempt not only for his younger brother, but also for his father. Although the older son had remained at home, he, too, had wandered to the far country just as surely as had his younger brother.

Where's God in the Pigsty?

If God is a being of grace and mercy, why would he have let his child get to the point of starving in a pigsty? If with our free will we choose to separate from our Source, we will suffer need, lack and impoverishment. God cannot enter the pigpen because God knows nothing of lack and limitation. God is abundance. You are in the pigsty because you have forgotten that God, while not in the pigsty, is nevertheless in you. This realization brings release. The door of the pigpen has always been open. You need only walk through it.

The older son, although not in a physical pigsty, nevertheless harbored a pigsty within his mind. His failure to recognize his abundance caused him to suffer as much lack and limitation as his brother had suffered. His father's words to him, "You are always with me. All I have is yours," speaks volumes to us. You need only—be still an instant—and return to the remembrance that you cannot be separated from God's love, abundance and eternal blessings. You can only think that you are. It is not the will of God that you live in a pigsty. It is God's will that you return home.

Only You Can Deprive Yourself

Both sons are prodigals—they wasted their inheritance. In separate ways they deprived themselves of their father's resources; they deprived themselves of God's love. And so do we.

As children—creations of God, we have been endowed with an inheritance: Love, sinlessness, perfection, knowledge and eternal truth. Each one of us is a treasure of God. But you, who are God's treasure, don't think you are valuable—you, who are God's treasure, don't think you are worthy. Why do we feel unworthy and not good enough? Every day we sell that robe, we drop the ring down the sewer, and we kick off our shoes.

You cannot understand that you are worthy and valuable; that you have something to offer other people until you realize that you are God's treasure—*you* are the blessed and beloved child in whom God is well pleased.

Lost or Found?

Let's take another look at the two sons. They both speak to us of living in a state of isolation, lack and limitation as a consequence of having separated in consciousness from the comfort of God's embrace.

The younger son speaks to us of our desire to run away and of our hunger to arise in consciousness and return to Love. The older son exemplifies how we leave home every day through our resentment and intolerance of other people. He might be more difficult to relate to because he shows us aspects of ourselves that we may not want to see. While the older son was certainly dutiful and responsible, he was also angry, bitter and resentful. The younger son judged and condemned himself, while the elder judged and condemned others. It doesn't matter whether we condemn other people or ourselves, with either attitude we remain lost. We remain lost because home is not a place of condemnation—home is Love.

The father gave the same inheritance to both his sons. The elder is just as much of a prodigal son as the younger because he too wasted his inheritance. Harboring resentment, the older son didn't recognize his true inheritance of his father's love and so instead, he felt deprived and envious of his brother. And I'll bet that the older son had never even asked for a party!

The younger son is better off because he left home and returned to the remembrance that he could not lose his divine inheritance. The older son, however, doesn't even know that he lives in a state of lack and limitation; he doesn't know that he, too, has squandered his true inheritance—he doesn't think he has a problem!

Many people live their lives this way: Thinking that because they are religious they have not strayed from home, but this is not necessarily true. Organized religion provides a set of rules, and it is thought that if one abides by those rules, then he or she is safe and godly. Spirituality on the other hand, is about cultivating a relationship with God—coming to know God as an internal Source of love, guidance, abundance and strength.

There are those who think that they have not left God, but nevertheless live their lives in worry, anger and fear—thinking that God is going to punish them or that the devil is out to get them. They are no closer to God than those they think of as sinners and runaways—they ran away too.

The two sons also teach us about pride and humility. The Bible tells us that God gives grace to the humble. In truth, God's grace is available to each and every one of us. It is only with humility that we receive it. The younger son came home with an attitude of humility—willing to be a servant. But pride kept the older son from receiving his brother with the same grace and love that their father had shown to both of them.

Ultimately, the two sons give us a choice: remain lost or become found. The younger son was lost, but in recognition of his lost state, he was found. We cannot truly become found until we recognize that we are lost. And what about the older son? Was he lost or found? Did he forgo his pride, enter the party and fellowship with his brother and his father? Or did he stay outside only to remain bitter and angry? What would you do?

The Father

We now come to the father who represents the universal Father/Mother/God of unfailing grace, love and abundance. The parable of the prodigal sons reveals to us that we are children who leave home and waste our inheritance; that we are children who condemn one another and ourselves. But it also reveals the Father/Mother/God within us that is the burning flame of love. We are rebellious children—but we are also Love itself.

We long to know, really know this mysterious God who we are told readily accepts us, and who embraces us with the warmth of enduring love. We come to know who and what God is as we allow our inner light to extend unconditional love to all of our brothers and sisters. The extension of God's love is the purpose of life here on earth. It is our purpose and our responsibility to grow into the Divine parent who extends grace and unconditional love to all of humanity.

And so, as you go about your life, recognize that in various ways you leave home many times, every single day. But in this moment—be still—home waits. Hasten there. For you are not lost, but found.

SHADOW CLUES

The shadow has been thought of as the dark self, the repressed self, the disowned self and the other self. But perhaps it is not a self at all. We live on this earth as two selves: The small, limited pretend self that we made with the ego; and the pure, perfect, powerful Self which was created by God. The ego self represses and disowns anything unacceptable to its ideal of what one should be in the world. The spiritual Self is our light—who and what we really are without the pretense of the ego in front of it.

"Shade" and "shadow" have similar definitions: "to screen or hide from view." Could it be then that the shadow lies between the two selves as a screen in our mind, hiding whatever we don't want to see? In this sense, the shadow isn't our darkness, it merely shades aspects of darkness and light already within.

Another definition of the word shadow is "a protector; an inseparable companion." How well that fits. The shadow is our constant companion, protecting us from seeing what we have relegated to the unconscious part of our mind. The shadow is a friend to the spiritual Self because as we bring awareness to the suppressed or denied aspects of ourselves, we can then accept and own them and thus approach wholeness. For the same reason, the shadow is an enemy to the pretend self because this self has no interest in becoming whole it merely yearns to "fit in."

Carl Jung said that he would rather be whole than good. Wholeness requires that we own all aspects of ourselves: The good as well as the bad, the beautiful as well as the ugly. The ego self does not want us to look at either the beautiful or the ugly, but the spiritual Self desires that we bring attention to both.

Lessons Learned From Dr. Jekyll

A story that exemplifies our struggle is *The Strange Case of Dr. Jekyll and Mr. Hyde*, by Robert Louis Stevenson.

Dr. Jekyll's problem was not that he was a bad man. It was not that he was so evil, but his moral aspirations were so high that even his little urges and desires seemed to him to be horrible. He said, "I had traveled one path my whole life, and it was the moral path."

Many people do not want to have anything to do with religion or spirituality because it brings them face to face with their fear and negative patterns. The ego tells us that we are supposed to love and forgive, all the time. Since few of us are capable of that, we end up with even more stuff to shove into our shadow.

We get angry and justify it with, "Of course I'm angry, look what he did!" When we learn that our anger isn't about what they did, but stems from within us, we may then feel more miserable than ever before, harboring not only anger, but also guilt.

You may be thinking at this point, 'I don't want to get into this spiritual stuff because it makes me feel so bad about myself!' This is what was happening to Dr. Jekyll. It wasn't that he was so bad, but he thought he was supposed to be a good, moral person, all the time.

He thought, 'Wouldn't it be wonderful if one could separate the dark, evil aspect of himself from the light, moral citizen?' He thought that it would dispel all the problems in life if one's dark side didn't have to worry about interference from the light side, and the light side didn't have to worry about the dark side screwing up their life. Dr. Jekyll, being a chemist, devised a potion that would separate his two selves. He actually went so far as to set up an apartment and bank account for Mr. Hyde to complete the separation.

"At first, my desires and my pleasures seemed undignified,"

said Dr. Jekyll. "But in the hands of Mr. Hyde they became monstrous!" Initially he was appalled by what Mr. Hyde was doing, but then he came to rationalize, 'It's him! It is Mr. Hyde who is doing those things, not me.' He came to take pleasure in some of Hyde's escapades and adventures.

Initially Dr. Jekyll reluctantly liked Mr. Hyde, but Mr. Hyde never liked Dr. Jekyll. Finally they came to the point of hating each other. Understand that they are two sides of the same person: The dark hating the light, the good citizen hating the criminal. Later in the story, Mr. Hyde began to overtake Dr. Jekyll. It was as if the dark side was slowly enveloping the light.

When Dr. Jekyll woke up one morning as Mr. Hyde, he realized that he was losing the balance of his soul. He had to make a choice between his moral, good self and his evil self. "I chose my good and moral self, but like many men, I found myself wanting in the strength to keep it."

Although Dr. Jekyll did choose his good self, in an hour of moral weakness, he again drank the potion and became Mr. Hyde. On that night he did a dastardly thing, he murdered someone held in high esteem. Dr. Jekyll was at wits end, 'Oh my God, what am I going to do now? I have become the worst of mankind! I am hunted! I am homeless! I am a known murderer!' Ultimately, Dr. Jekyll felt that escape would come only through death.

Dr. Jekyll's story is profound in that it reveals the consequences of attempting to separate the various aspects of our being. Dr. Jekyll was unable to look at the facets that didn't fit his ideal of a good, moral person. In his attempt to separate these facets, he destroyed himself in the process.

The Gospel of Thomas says that if you bring forth what is within you, what you bring forth will save you. If you do not bring forth what is within you, what you do not bring forth will destroy you.

So, how do we bring forth what is within us? How can we recognize our shadow?

Shadow Clues

The way we project outward from that which is within was introduced in the chapter "Choose Another Street." Here, we will delve into the idea of projection more deeply. Carl Jung first coined the term "shadow," his observation being that it is essentially all that we harbor in our unconscious. It is this unconscious aspect of our mind that does the projecting, thus we are usually unaware of our projections. Our very lives, however, provide the clues.

As you delve into this chapter, imagine that you are a detective about to set out on an investigation to find out what is in your shadow. Every time you see the word "clue," you might want to make a note of the thoughts that come up in regard to that clue.

Shadows in Relationships

Our reactions to other people must be looked at closely. We not only project onto other people the things we don't like about ourselves, but also the qualities considered "good" but that we have denied as even being part of us.

You may have heard that what you don't like about another person reflects what you don't like about yourself. While this can certainly be true it's not that simple because, we also project negative emotions onto other people because they are so *different* from us.

An observation that someone is arrogant is not necessarily a shadow projection. But if their behavior drives you crazy or even mildly irritates you, then it is. This still doesn't mean that you are arrogant, but obviously something about their behavior triggers negative reactions. On the other hand, if you admire or respect someone that again is not a shadow projection, but if you overvalue the person, place him or her on a pedestal, for instance, then it is. Perhaps you view the person as a savior in the sense that he or she might fix or complete you.

Romantic relationships are rife with shadow projections. Call to mind such a relationship, and reflect on the qualities that you love most about him or her. Next, call to mind his or her flaws. Especially in the early stages of romance, one might exclaim, "The person I love has no flaws!" If you are in love with a person who has no flaws, either you met him over the weekend or you are not in love with a real person! More than likely, you are in love with your projections. You may have projected the qualities of your perfect mate onto another person. Consequently, you don't see him or her as they really are, you see your "perfect mate." You might also project such ideals of perfection onto children, parents, friends, or anyone else you claim to love. Have you noticed that after awhile few people live up to your ideal?

It is unfortunate that human beings frequently invalidate other human beings. Unconsciously, we project our weaknesses and flaws onto other people, and we also project our repressed gifts and talents onto them. We then either judge them for their weaknesses or we invalidate their gifts.

Awareness Exercise

This would be a good place to stop and make a list of some of the people you dislike, overvalue, love and/or invalidate. Next to each name, write the qualities that evoke a negative reaction or a positive response. As you begin to bring awareness to the reactions and responses you have about other people, you will gain many clues about yourself. Everything you see out there is a projection of something within you.

Shadows on the News

The news media has become a stage—parading the shadow for the world to see. How we react to the news can give us many personal shadow *clues*. Try this: The next time you read or watch the news, attempt to go beyond judgment of good or bad, right or wrong, moral or immoral, and instead bring awareness to your reactions. I heard that you will know you have advanced spiritually if you can watch the news without reacting to anything on it, good or bad. I have a long way to go! And you?

> **Awareness Exercise**
> *Here, you may want to reflect on some of the news stories that really push your buttons. What did they have to do with? Think about the judgments and criticisms you make about a particular "group"; i.e. race, religion, political party, gender, or about particular public people. Ask yourself what it is about that group or individual that disturbs you so much. Here again, you will find many shadow **clues.***

Shadows in the Almighty Dollar

We can find many shadow *clues* in our individual and collective projections about money. On a collective level, money has become a god in contemporary society. Those with an excess of money are held in high esteem based on that fact alone. Consequently, money has become something that many people use to define their self-worth, which is why we see so much emphasis on materialism these days. Materialism is preoccupation with material objects, comforts and considerations, as opposed to spiritual or intellectual values. In a materialistic society we are valued for what we have rather than for who we are.

Who hasn't heard that money is the root of all evil. Money, however, is just something we use to pay for things—it's not good or bad. What we attach to money can present a problem for us. There is nothing wrong with having or desiring money. God's kingdom is one of abundance. Living with a sense of abundance has to do with recognition and appreciation that you already have whatever you need.

> **Awareness Exercise**
> *Stop here and note if you resent those who have money? Do you snub those who don't have as much money as you do? Do you try to increase your sense of self-worth with money and material possessions? Or do you simply enjoy the necessities, comforts and pleasures that money affords you? Do you share your money? As you bring awareness to your attitudes and beliefs about money and how you use money, you will gain **clues** to the unconscious thoughts that created those attitudes and beliefs.*

Shadows in the Car

When I was in my early 20s, I read that one's true personality comes out behind the wheel of a car. I was horrified because I became a banshee in the car. My shadow reigned! What is it about being behind the wheel of a car that seems to bring out the worst in so many of us? It's as if we take the actions of an anonymous person in another vehicle personally. Why is it that we can and often do, let another person who is totally unaware of our existence put us in a state of total agitation by performing a wrong move in the car? All I know for sure is that it presents *clues* to the shadow.

If you frequently get angry while driving, this is a clue that on some level, you were already angry before you got into the car. You might be thinking, 'But no. I'm angry because that guy pulled in front of me!' The actions of other people cannot evoke anger unless anger is already within. When this is the case, it doesn't take much. Have you noticed? Although I have come a long way in this regard, the freeway can still present one of my greater spiritual challenges.

My husband and I sometimes engage in a little tiff over the use of the horn. I view the horn in my car as an extension of myself—it speaks to the person in front of me when I can't jump out of the car and speak for myself. On the other hand, my husband won't beep the horn even when someone is backing into him! "What do you think it's there for?" I exclaim. My husband is much less confrontational than I am, so I can only gather that he views beeping his horn as an act of confrontation. Neither way is right or wrong—simply be aware of the shadow *clues* to be gained from your behavior in the car.

Sex and the Shadow

A discussion of the shadow must include sex. Sexual shadows pervade on a collective as well as an individual level. Sex education in our schools, and in many homes, generally teach only the risks. Not that the risks are unimportant, but what about the beautiful aspects of sexuality that occurs between two mutually consenting adults who love and care for each other? I'm not saying that we should tell our kids, "Sex is great! Go for it!" A balanced presentation of the subject, however, is important. Reflect on what you were taught about sex and what you would have liked to have been told about it.

For many of us, the very idea of sex and its place in our lives has become confusing, to say the least. Therefore, it is not surprising that we have so many sexual issues in our shadow. There is probably more shame in the area of sexuality than in any other aspect of our lives.

The word "shame" is defined as "the painful feeling of having done, thought or experienced something improper." With that definition in mind, can any one of us say that we have not experienced feelings of shame in regard to our sexuality? It is probably safe to say that there isn't an adult on this planet who doesn't harbor sexual secrets of one kind or another. If you reflect on the things you wouldn't want to reveal to another human being— they probably have to do with sex.

Organized religion hasn't done us any favors in the area of sexuality. In *I Come As A Brother*, Bartholomew says, "On some level, your parents told you that if you had sex before you were married, God was going to get you. And you believed it! Not enough not to do it, just enough to feel guilty about it."

Guilt and shame over our sexuality causes us to deny our true feelings and desires regarding it. We then either project our guilt based attitudes and feelings onto other people, or we act them out.

In *The Mystery of Marriage*, Mike Mason wrote:

Surely it was God's full intention for the physical joining of two people to be one of the mountaintop experiences in life. One of those summit points of both physical and mystical rapture in which God might overshadow His people in love; might come down among them and be most intimately and powerfully revealed. How horribly tragic, therefore, that it is here at this very point, that some people have succeeded in descending to some of the most abysmal levels of human degradation. Yet what a high price is paid for the least cheapening of a gift so full of beauty and grace and power!

Sex is sacred ground. It is a place where humans may turn themselves into animals or else may begin to be transformed into the children of God. It is more conspicuously than anywhere else, the place where the angel and the animal in humanity meet face to face and engage in mortal struggle.

Shadows in Religion

A staunchly religious, elderly black man moved to a new town and went over to join the local church. As he talked with the minister, it became clear to him that the minister really didn't want him there. He finally said, "I think I'll go home and pray about it, and then I'll come back in a few days."

"Yes, why don't you do that," the minister replied. The man came back a few days later and the minister asked, "Well, did God give you a message?"

"Yes, He did. He told me to give it up. God said, 'I've been trying to get in that church for ten years, and even I can't get in there!'"[24]

In the introduction to *The World Treasury of Modern Religious Thought*, Jaroslav Pelikan writes, "Religious belief is notorious for encouraging a sense of us against them." Rather than letting our religious or spiritual beliefs bring us into union with one another and with God, we often use them to further separate. Much of religion is of the ego, being based on fear, judgment and exclusivity. God, however, is not a god of exclusion, but one of unconditional love.

I frequently listen to a particular Christian minister whose teachings I really enjoy and gain a lot of growth from. But I find it interesting when in one breath she talks about other Christians who condemn her for one thing or another, and then in the next breath she condemns New Age spirituality or teachings that are not Christian. We all do this on some level. It is important that we bring awareness to our judgment and criticism of other religions or spiritual paths.

> **Awareness Exercise**
> *Do you use your religious or spiritual beliefs to feel superior to other people? Or do you use them to condemn or judge other people or yourself? These are shadow **clues**. Looking at these unconscious beliefs and attitudes can perhaps return us to the remembrance that God loves each one of us equally regardless of race, religion, gender or sexuality.*

What about Hypocrisy?

Another way we can find shadow clues is to look at the people we deem as hypocrites. Hypocrisy is a pretense of having virtues, moral principles or religious beliefs that one does not really possess. Those who speak or write about spiritual principles, not to mention those of us who try to live them, are no less human than anyone else. I have mastered spiritual principles enough to effect great changes in my life. I have mastered spiritual principles enough to effectively teach them. But by no means am I a spiritual master!

Let's face it, until the day we leave this earth, most of us will judge others, feel hurt or get angry. If a person is behaving in a way that you might deem hypocritical, you may be unaware of the fact that he or she used to behave that way all the time and now has more control. In my own life, after those times when I've behaved the ugliest, through looking at my behavior and forgiving myself and the others involved, I often come to a greater sense of peace within myself.

Embracing your shadow is not as much about transcending your negative patterns as it is about bringing awareness to them. You grow, not through denying or repressing your darkness, but by looking at it. The only way you can come to inner peace is by bringing awareness to the shadow clues in all aspects of your life. As long as you deny your negative patterns you will experience inner turmoil. We all make mistakes and will continue to do so. Such mistakes are not evidence of our hypocrisy, but of our humanity.

To paraphrase George Orwell, "Yes, I will admit that a saint probably shouldn't drink, smoke, cuss or have sex, but I don't think any human should aspire to sainthood." I agree! Religious dogma and doctrine will not change you. The law of, I should do this, or I should be that, will not change you. You are changed as you bring awareness to your negative patterns, and then ask the Holy Spirit to look at them with you.

Become an Observer

We must stop reacting blindly to the people and situations in our lives and instead step back and observe our reactions. Such observations can give us the clues that facilitate self-awareness, which leads to self-knowledge and finally to self-acceptance. It is okay to have compulsions, patterns and secrets that you won't tell anybody about, but if you continue to deny them to yourself they will emerge, and usually unexpectedly. They may erupt in illness, neurosis, sexual dysfunction, a midlife crisis, or in the conflicts you have every day. In this way, they are saying, "Look at me!"

There Is Gold in Your Shadow

Carl Jung observed that the shadow is ninety-percent pure gold. When you begin to look at your projections, positive and negative—

you mine your gold. I got into spirituality to gain things from the outer world like more money, better relationships, and the like. But along the way I had to look at myself and through doing so, I found gifts and talents I didn't know I had. There is no way I could have presented these words to you unless I had been willing to do some investigative and healing work with my numerous shadow clues.

Remember that the shadow is a friend to your spiritual Self. Since it is this Self that desires to extend itself creatively and abundantly into the world, you must bring awareness to all the ways that you might be denying that Self. You can only do this with willingness to look at the shadow projections that serve to keep your true Self from your awareness.

Bringing It All Together

If you haven't already done so, at this point you might want to go back through the previous sections of this chapter and reflect on the shadow *clues* that speak to you. Then what?

Acceptance

"You always talk about working on ourselves, but what about accepting ourselves as we are?" I was asked. Coming to an acceptance of yourself is what the work of integrating the shadow is about, which you may have noticed, is no easy task!

In the *Phaedrus*, Plato likened our earthly dilemma to driving a chariot with two horses: *One is a white horse, gallant and gentle, constantly looking upward to a divine world it aspires to return to. The other a dark horse, unruly and vicious, obstinately plunging downward dragging the chariot behind him.*

Plato eloquently describes the spiritual Self and the ego self. One looks constantly toward the light, while the other plunges toward the darkness. Have you observed these opposing forces within you? Remember that the shadow is an unconscious attempt to deny darkness and light within. Without an acknowledgement and an acceptance of these opposing inner forces, you cannot approach wholeness.

Self-acceptance does not mean that you condone negative or self-destructive behaviors, but that you become aware of them. If you continually make excuses for such behavior, you look to something outside of you as the cause of your circumstances. Outside appearances are merely effect, not cause. Once you come to recognize that something in you is perpetuating the circumstances, then and only then can you begin to heal.

Becoming Conscious

The caterpillar enters the chrysalis, and through a mysterious inner process, transforms into a butterfly. But what if the caterpillar called out from the chrysalis, "I'm not coming out. I don't want to come out. I don't want to be a butterfly. I don't know what it is like to be a butterfly. I am happy being a caterpillar. I'm staying right here!" Eventually the chrysalis would shrivel up, and the caterpillar would die. That is what we're doing. The caterpillar is asleep in the chrysalis, and we are asleep in this world. It's as if we are in the chrysalis exclaiming, "I don't want to spread my wings! I don't want to be powerful. I don't want to be free. I want to stay a caterpillar. I want to stay unconscious!"

With willingness to become the butterfly, you essentially say to the universe, "I want to spread my wings. I want to wake up. I want to know who I am." The butterfly is the highest expression of the caterpillar, and it is a symbol for the soul. The spiritual, innocent part of you is your highest expression, and you are meant to be that in the world, but not just that. Despite what the ego tells you, no one can be just that, as this favorite poem by Kabir says:

Friend, please tell me about this world
I hold to, and keep spinning out.
I gave up clothes with seams in them,
And wore a robe,
But I noticed one day that the robe
 was made of expensive cloth.
So I got rid of the robe, and bought some burlap.
But then I noticed that I threw it elegantly over my left shoulder.
I pulled back my sexual longings,
and now I discover that I'm angry a lot!
I gave up rage, and now I notice
that I am greedy all day!
 I worked hard at dissolving the greed,
 and now I'm proud of myself.
When the mind wants to break its link with the world
it still holds on to one thing.
Kabir says: Listen my friend,
there are very few that find the path!

Ask For Help

You cannot do this work alone. Don't try to. You have help, guidance and strength within you at all times. You need only ask for it. The Holy Spirit is our Comforter, Healer, Guide, Strengthener, Friend, and in my opinion, the Ultimate Therapist! Before I recognized this powerful, loving Presence in my life, I gained insight to my negative patterns through books, tapes, therapists or whatever. But it wasn't until I came into relationship with the ultimate therapist that I experienced healing in various areas of my life.

You Are Not Healed Alone

As you approach wholeness you bring other people along with you. As you integrate and accept your shadow, you can then begin to accept the shadow in others. Such an acceptance of yourself and thus other people, brings you to healing. You are not healed alone. Your healing affects the lives of others. You glimpse enlightenment when you recognize that we are all perfect, and we are all imperfect. The paradox of human life is that we must come to honor our imperfection within our perfection.

And so, as you go about your life, don't be like Dr. Jekyll. Instead, be willing to embrace the light and dark, the saint and sinner, the good citizen and criminal within your own heart.[25] Thus you come to know yourself, accept yourself, and yes, even love yourself.

Many of us grew up with *The Wizard of Oz*. Revisiting it as an adult, I was struck by how it speaks of our very human yearning to return to our true home.[26]

> During a horrific cyclone Dorothy's house spins into Munchkin land. It drops to the earth, landing on and killing the Wicked Witch of the East. The Munchkins are overjoyed by this turn of events because the Witch has held them in bondage for many years. She gave daily sermons filled with hellfire and damnation—keeping them enslaved through guilt and the fear of God. Her death set them free. They happily make jokes about her. The best one: "That old Witch was giving such a great hellfire sermon that she really brought down the house!"[27]
>
> As Dorothy and her dog Toto exit the house, she is horrified to find that she has killed the witch. The Munchkins, however, elevate her to living sainthood. They find Toto merely annoying. The Munchkins curiously gather around her asking where she came from. "I come from Kansas. I just want to go home!" exclaims Dorothy. At that moment, Glinda, the Good Witch of the North, makes her appearance. She goes over to the Witch of the East and removes her shoes. (By the way, in the book, they are silver shoes!) Glinda gives Dorothy the silver shoes, and tells her they are magical.

"But I just want to go home!" Dorothy cries again.

"Then you must go see the Wizard in Emerald City," replies Glinda.

"But how do I get there?"

"You must walk. It is a long and difficult journey through a country that is sometimes pleasant, and sometimes dark and terrible, but never fear because if you call me I will be there to guide you and lend you my strength."

Dorothy, somewhat relieved, puts on the silver shoes, picks up Toto and sets off down the yellow brick road.

The Homeward Journey

Have you ever felt like an alien? Dorothy symbolizes the child within who seeks home and knows that she is alien here. Like Dorothy, at some point you too will embark on a journey because the memory of home haunts you, calling you to return. As you travel, don't forget that you are never alone. Glinda represents the Inner Presence that gives you guidance and strength for the very asking.

Dorothy sets out on her journey and before long a voice calls out to her. She looks around and sees a scarecrow. The Scarecrow asks where she is going. "I'm off to see the Wizard," she replies. "I am going to ask him to send me home."

"Well as you can see, I'm just a stuffed man. I don't have any brains. Do you think the Wizard would give me brains?" Dorothy thinks it over and asks him to join her on the journey. "What a grand idea!" exclaims the Scarecrow. They set off together.

Later they come across a man made of tin. As they tell him their story he asks, "Do you think the Wizard would give me a heart?"

"I don't see why not," the Scarecrow replies. "I am going to ask him for brains."

"Oh, I have had them both," replies the Tin Man. "I've had brains and I've had a heart. I have learned that it is much more important to have a heart."

"Why do you say that?" asks the Scarecrow.

The Tin Man proceeds to tell them his tale. "I used to be a woodcutter. I fell in love with a beautiful Munchkin girl. She lived with an old woman who didn't want her to marry anyone. The old woman went to the Wicked Witch of the East for help. The witch agreed to help her, and put a curse on my ax. One day, as I was out chopping wood, I chopped off my right leg! But luckily my best friend was a tinsmith and he made me a new leg. Later, while again chopping wood, I cut off my other leg. This went on until all of my body parts were cut off! So now you know how I became a man made of tin. Even so, I thought I had outfoxed the witch and the old woman because I was doing fine. Alas! One day, as I was chopping wood, the ax turned on me, splitting my heart right in two. To my misfortune, the tinsmith couldn't make me a new heart.

"I have suffered many losses in my life, but the greatest was that of my heart. When I lost my heart, I lost all love for the Munchkin girl. While in love I was the happiest man on earth. So brains may be nice, but without a heart you cannot be happy."

Dorothy and the Scarecrow are saddened by the Tin Man's story. They ask him to join them, and so he does.

Walking along the yellow brick road laughing and having a grand old time, suddenly they hear a ferocious roar. The Scarecrow and the Tin Man run for cover; Toto barks. Dorothy spots a lion and runs up to him shouting, "How dare you! How dare you scare my friends like that! Just who do you think you are?"

The Lion quivers and replies, "I am so sorry. Who do I think I am? Well everyone thinks that I am King of the Beasts. But really, I am a coward. I have found that if I roar very loudly, man and beast will run away. And of course I let them go. For if any had tried to fight me, I'd run myself. I'm a coward. I am just a coward. Look at me. I'm afraid of you, and you're just a mere little girl."

Dorothy feels sorry for the lion and says, "We are off to see the Wizard, the wonderful Wizard of Oz. The Scarecrow is going to ask for brains, the Tin Man, a heart. I am going to ask him to send me home. Maybe he will give you some courage."

"Do you think he would?" the Lion asked.

"We can only ask," Dorothy replied. "You know what it says in the scriptures, 'Ask and you shall receive.' All we can do is ask."

Challenges on the Journey

As the foursome travel the yellow brick road, they meet with many challenges and difficulties. Not unlike those that we encounter on our journey home. I read a wonderful parable about challenges:

A bank robber is killed when he attempts to escape with the loot. He wakes up to light and harp music. He sees a man in a white suit who seems to be in charge, and assuming that he had died and gone to Heaven, he walks up to him.

The White Suit says, "While you're here you get to do the three things you love the most." "Great! I love to gamble. I love to be with beautiful women. And I love to rob banks!" He is told to "Go for it." And he does!

As months go by, he begins to notice something very strange. Every time he gambles, he wins. Every beautiful woman he lays eyes on falls instantly madly in love with him. And every time he robs a bank, he escapes unharmed with all the loot. This was all fabulous at first, but he is soon bored. He approaches the White Suit and says, "This is the dullest place I've ever been. Who'd ever have thought Heaven would be such a boring place?" With an evil smile spreading across his face, White Suit replies, "What made you think this was Heaven?"

We seem to think that life would be joyous if we live a charmed life absent of problems. But while it is true that our challenges and difficulties can be a nuisance, they also give us the opportunity to take a different course. If your life had been "oh so wonderful," would you be reading this book? Relationship problems, illnesses, money problems—without them would you have sought higher truth? And even though the search for higher truth can be a challenge, there is nothing more fulfilling than beginning to seek and find your Self.

Dorothy and company overcome numerous challenges on their journey—eventually arriving to Emerald City. They are thrilled and excited to finally be there. At the gates they are given green lenses and told to wear them at all times. They find it hilarious that everyone and everything in the city is green.

After waiting many days they are finally granted an

interview with the Wizard. They enter a huge dark room. Suddenly, they hear a loud, thunderous noise. The Lion whimpers in fear and hides behind Dorothy's skirt. The Scarecrow and the Tin Man act nonchalant and Toto, of course, barks.

The Wizard appears as a great head, seeming to descend from the ceiling. He bellows, "I will grant you your wishes. But first, you must kill the Wicked Witch of the West! KILL HER! Bring me her broomstick to prove you have done it. When you return I will give you what you want. NOW, BE GONE!"

"Oh my God!" exclaims Dorothy, "I feel bad enough for killing the Witch of the East. Now I am being asked to kill her sister. No! No! No! I cannot possibly do such a thing!" They despondently set off on their journey, not knowing where to go or what to do because they are not too thrilled about finding, let alone killing the Wicked Witch of the West.

Soon, they find themselves outside the Witch's castle where they are captured. The Witch sits in her chamber peering into her looking glass. "What a cliché, the witch with her looking glass. Young Dorothy reminds me of myself at her age. Ah...as I peer into my mirror, what do I see but myself? And that is the curse!"

Your Life Is a Mirror

Just like the witch, you may initially see this idea as a curse. But it is really a gift because your life merely reflects what is going on inside of you. A constant lack of money reveals an internal consciousness of scarcity and lack. Relationship after relationship that ends dismally points to fears of intimacy and love. Conversely, an abundant experience in many aspects of one's life also reflects an internal consciousness. Your life reveals your inner state of consciousness.

Dorothy and her friends are captured. Dorothy is brought before the Witch.

"Take off those shoes!" demands the Witch.

"I would be happy to," replies Dorothy, "but I can't get them off."

"I know you came here to kill me. I know all that is going on around here, and I know that you came here to kill me!"

"I did not come here to kill you." cries Dorothy in shock and terror. "I was grief-stricken at killing your sister."

"But didn't the Wizard send you here to kill me?" asks the Witch.

"Yes, the Wizard sent me here to kill you, but that is not why I came."

"So, why did you come?"

Dorothy hangs her head and quietly replies, "I came to ask for your forgiveness. I feel so terrible for killing your sister. I can't forgive myself for it. I would be so happy if you could find it in your heart to forgive me."

The Witch is blown away by this idea. Forgiveness? Right! However, she is intrigued. "Well my sister and I really didn't get along all that well anyway. We had very different views about life."

At that moment, her broom falls into the fireplace and catches on fire. As a spark of fire catches the hem of the Witch's skirt, Dorothy screams, "Oh, my God, I must save her! I must save her!" She looks around, finds a bucket of water, and casts it at the Witch. To her surprise and horror, the witch shrivels before her eyes and melts away. "Oh my God!" Dorothy cries, "I have killed two witches!"

Light Dissolves Darkness

The Witch represents the ego—our unforgiveness, thoughts that attack; our hatred, fear and guilt. But it's not that we must kill, conquer or control the ego, we need only shine light on it. Light is understanding, forgiveness and love. We call on the light when we ask the Higher Presence to look at our darkness with us. Dorothy asked the Witch for forgiveness, and in the presence of Dorothy's light the Witch dissolved. When you are willing to see a person or situation from the higher perception of forgiveness and love, in that moment you enter the light.

Dorothy grabs the charred broomstick and runs to set her friends free. They travel back to Emerald City for another interview with the Wizard. They present the broomstick to the Wizard and once again ask him to grant their wishes. He refuses. Feeling very upset and betrayed by the Wizard, they turn to leave. Toto runs over to a curtain, pulls it back, and exposes a little old man.

Live Authentically

We also have this curtain in our mind. We present a false persona to the world, afraid of being exposed. Not only are we afraid to stand forth as who we really are, we cannot because our very fear blocks our remembrance of our true Self. It takes courage to authentically *be* in a world that does not value authenticity—in a world that values "Let's pretend." Most of us can relate to the Wizard being exposed if we feel that we have something to hide. We must look at our fear with the vision of our Spirit. It is this

Internal Presence that is genuine and real. As we recognize our spirit, we begin to extend from that place of light.

> The Wizard has certainly not been authentic, and after being found out he says, "I guess I must tell you my story. I landed here many years ago in a balloon, and of course, since I descended from the sky the Munchkins thought I was a wizard. So I built this city and called it Emerald City. I made everyone wear green glasses so that everything would look green, but now they have worn them for so long they think everything is green."

Through Which Lens Do You View The World?

It seems that we wear either rose colored glasses (denial) or contaminated lenses (fear). We rarely view the world from our true internal vision. We see what we believe is there. When we are asked to take off those lenses, we resist. In what ways do you resist taking off the lenses of denial or fear? You can only move out of these patterns as you bring awareness to them.

> The Scarecrow asks the Wizard, "Do you mean to tell me that you aren't really a wizard?"
>
> "No, I'm afraid I am not a wizard. I'm a really good man, but I am not a very good wizard. For so many years I lived in terror of the witches, and so I created an evil persona so that everyone would be afraid of me. And it worked."
>
> "Wait a minute! Wait a minute! Let me get this straight," says the Scarecrow. "You are not going to give me brains?"
>
> "*You had it all the time.* The longer you live, the more experiences you have. Your experience combined with

your knowledge equals wisdom. I have spies all around these parts. Throughout your journey here, wasn't it you who came up with all the great ideas that saved your companions time and time again?"

"Yes, come to think of it, I guess I did come up with quite a few good ideas."

"See, *you had it all the time.* You need only to believe in yourself." says the Wizard. The Scarecrow agrees to work on it.

"Well, what about me?" asks the Tin Man, "I need a heart."

"I watched you too," says the Wizard. "Wasn't it you who wept at every unkind act? Isn't it true that you would rather die than be mean to, or kill anyone?"

Puzzled, the Tin Man replies, "Yes, I guess I do have that weakness."

"On no!" exclaims the Wizard. "That is not a weakness my friend, but a very great strength. Kindness to others is a deed of greatness. I could implant a heart into your breast, but that would not make you love. Look around you. All human beings have a heart, but how many of them extend love? How many of them exhibit your quiet kindness and strength?"

"A really good point." says the Tin Man, "Are you saying that I am already loving?"

"Yes, that is what I'm saying. *You had it all the time.* You don't need a physical heart to love. The capacity to love is inherent in who and what you are. You can never lose love, but you can lose your awareness of it."

"How can I ever thank you?" asks the Tin Man.

"Be who you are. That will be enough."

The Lion steps forward and says, "All right! Okay! I

understand that the Scarecrow was already wise; and I understand that the Tin Man was already loving, but I am still a coward. I'm afraid of everything!"

"I watched you too," said the Wizard. "Yes, it was the Scarecrow who came up with all those great ideas, but you were the one who had the courage to implement them."

"Yes that's true, but I was still afraid."

"Everyone is afraid. Courage is transcending your fear, if only for a moment, to help yourself or someone else. There is no one who is unafraid in the face of danger. True courage is found in facing the danger even though you are afraid. You have done that my friend. You need only believe in yourself, to have confidence in yourself. You are courageous. You are one of the most courageous beings I have ever met."

"I am?" asks the Lion in disbelief.

"Yes you are," replies the Wizard. "*You had it all the time.*"

The Wizard decides that he is ready to leave Emerald City. He offers to take Dorothy home in his balloon. As they prepare to leave, the balloon takes off without her.

"Oh God! What am I going to do now?" she cries.

Glinda (God's female impersonator) arrives on the scene. "I can help you. All you have to do is click your heels together three times and say, 'I want to go home, I want to go home, I want to go home.'"

"That's all I have to do?" asks Dorothy.

"Yes, that is all you have to do," Glinda replies. "Home is within you, *it was there all the time.* There is no such thing as a wizard. All the power you will ever need, any questions you will ever have, the answers are already within."

"Why didn't you tell me that to start with?" asks an incredulous Dorothy.

"You wouldn't have believed me. Some things you must discover on your own."

What's The Truth?

What or who have you made into your wizard? Your boss, mate, teachers, religion, parents, friends, or your bank account? You must seek your own answers. You must listen for them. All the answers you will ever need are found within.

We are like the Scarecrow when we think that we are not smart enough, educated enough, or that we are foolish or inept. And we are like the Tin Man when we perceive life through our mistaken attitudes and perceptions, rather than with our heart. We are like the Lion, when we roar and screech scaring everyone away, only to hide from them our own fear. And we are like Dorothy, yearning to go home.

Like them, *you have it all, all the time.* You have a mind with which you can choose again; a heart that speaks to you of love. You can face any and all of life's difficulties with courage that comes from God. And home rests within you.

You Have Everything You Need

Who teaches us the most in this story? Toto! He was the only being that didn't need anything from the Wizard because he knew that he already had everything. Dogs are happy because they live totally in the present. Your dog doesn't sit around lamenting, "Man! I just can't believe what that poodle did to me last week!" When you open your heart to this moment, you find that you have whatever you need—within.

And so, as you go about your life, remember that you find your way home one step at a time, receiving exactly what you need when you need it. *The Wizard of Oz* is a story about returning home, a place you never left. It is about recognizing what you already have and are. Once you return to this remembrance, you then extend your Self into the world. Enjoy!

5 MOVING FORWARD

Help me, O God,
to listen to what it is
that makes my heart glad
and to follow where it leads.

– Ken Gire, Windows of the Soul

———————————————

I don't know what your destiny will
be, but I do know one thing; the only
ones among you who will be happy
are those who have sought and
found how to serve.

– Albert Schweitzer

CONSCIOUS CREATIVITY

The universe is constantly in the process of creation. You participate in this on-going creation on two levels: The way in which you create your life through the power of choice; and through the extension of your creative gifts into the world. These two levels are interdependent because once you choose to express your creative gifts, you move forward to create a life filled with joy and purpose, and then go on to serve the universe from that higher level of being.

For the first half of my life I rarely thought about creativity and when I did, I associated it with those who are talented in the Arts. But I have learned that creativity is not just about the expression of a gift or talent, it comes into play in every aspect of our lives. Our greatest gifts often emerge from the healing of our deepest emotional wounds. After years of working to heal my anger through forgiveness, I saw my anger transmuted into a passion for spirituality.

Miraculously, I also began to recognize my creative gifts, and then extended those gifts through speaking and writing on spiritual principles. As I did this, I was led to further emotional healing. Because my newfound creativity took me deep within myself, in a sense, creativity became a spiritual path for me as well. As you delve into emotional and spiritual healing, you come into your highest creativity.

Crisis and Creativity

The crisis points in our lives can be opportunities that bring us to our highest creative expression. In *Grace and Grit*, Ken Wilbur relates the spiritual and healing journey he and his wife, Treya, endured and embraced in the midst of her five-year battle with cancer. Treya had kept journals of her experience, and before she died, she told Ken that he would need them. When he read them, he knew he had to offer them to the world, and *Grace and Grit* was born.

In a review of this book, a woman with cancer wrote: "Nobody worked on herself more or was more spiritual than Treya Wilber, and yet she still died." The woman went on to make disparaging comments about several spiritual teachers who teach responsibility and empowerment in the face of illness. Although she acknowledged that the book had profoundly inspired her, she had missed the point. Treya Wilber may have died, but through her journals and her husband Ken an inspirational book was written which has helped many people live a fuller life. No one could have done it quite the way they did.

Inspirational authors Louise Hay and Susan Jeffers, among countless others, have used their experiences with cancer to heal themselves and also to inspire and empower other people.

After the death of his young son, Rabbi Harold Kushner wrote, *When Bad Things Happen to Good People*, a beautiful and inspiring book that affirms life.

Richard Gayton recounts his journey from despair to forgiveness in his book, *The Forgiving Place*, written after his wife was killed.

Mothers Against Drunk Drivers (MADD) was creatively formed after a mother lost her child in an accident involving a drunk driver.

After her divorce, I read that Sue Grafton was so angry at her husband that she wanted to kill him. Instead, she used that energy to write a mystery novel, *A Is For Alibi*.

Through the transcendence of his own addiction, Bill Wilson, the founder of Alcoholics Anonymous, was able to help thousands of people return to living lives of meaning and purpose.

Although such examples abound in our world, they often go unrecognized. The crisis points in your life can enable you to give birth to your creative gifts, and your authentic Self. You may not have "created" all the things that occur in your life, but you do have a part in creating a new life in how you respond to them.

Everything that has ever happened to you was necessary to help you fulfill your highest destiny. Everything that has happened in your life can lead to serving others in a unique way. In the midst of pain and despair, ask for higher understanding and healing. Ask that it may be used in highest service to others and your Self. Choose to create from your pain, rather than choosing to be victimized by it. You can choose to let your experiences limit or liberate you. The ego keeps you imprisoned in pain and despair.

You Are Unique

There is a plan in this universe and you are part of it. No one else can fulfill your part exactly like you can because nobody else looks at the world in quite the same way. If all wrote a book on spirituality, every one would be different. If we all painted a picture, they would be different too. We would plant a garden differently, and raise our children differently—do not let the fear that you have nothing original to offer get in the way. Originality comes from the extension of your authentic Self. Only you can limit your creativity. Such limitation, however, is not God's will.

Creativity and Love Go Hand In Hand

At its most profound level, creativity is an extension of your love. To create is to love. Love and forgiveness become your highest creative acts because the extension of those energies can literally transform your life. When you forgive the people who you feel have hurt you, when you bring understanding and compassion to those who you feel are so different than yourself, you come from your highest level of service and creativity.

Your only function on this earth is to practice the art of love and forgiveness. Once you begin to practice this art, you will experience the emergence of your creative gifts. You will return to the remembrance that there is something you must do. When you withhold these gifts from the world, you withhold yourself from your Self, other people and God.

Masculine and Feminine Energies

The feminine energy contains the characteristics of intuition, creativity, being, receptivity, nurturing and compassion. The characteristics of masculine energy are: Logic, focus, extension, doing, action and assertiveness. The energy of God encompasses all of these characteristics.

In *The Art of Living Consciously*, Nathaniel Branden wrote:

An interesting study was done of a group of men and women who had been identified as highly creative by their peers. When this creative group was tested, it was found that the men, while in no way being unmasculine, exhibited many traits conventionally associated with femininity, such as high sensitivity, an aesthetic orientation, and so on. And the women tested, while in no way unfeminine, were found to have many traits conventionally associated with masculinity, such as self-assertiveness, strong goal-orientation, and the like.

My own explanation of this phenomenon is that creative people tend to be more respectful of their inner signals and as a consequence, tend to develop more multifaceted personalities. They do not slash away and repress whatever aspects of the self do not fit with conventional male and female stereotypes. They allow themselves to hear more of their inner music. In this respect, they live more consciously, although in other areas they may not.

It is true that many men are not open to their creativity because of repressed or denied feminine energy; while conversely, many women may be receptive to their creative ideas and inspirations, but have not sufficiently recognized the masculine energy in order to deliver those ideas to fruition. In order to express and thereby extend your inherent creative gifts, you must become aware of the masculine and feminine energies within. Balance of these energies is important because creativity is just as much about receiving as it is about doing. You receive your insights, ideas and intuitions through the receptive energy of the feminine. Yet it is the masculine energy that enables you to act on your ideas, insights and intuitions.

Give Birth to Your Ideas
In order to give birth to a child, the feminine must receive the seed of the masculine. Within this process you are not so much creating as allowing creation to occur through you. You may not have asked for it, yet something has chosen you, rather than you choosing it. Our creative gifts, just like our children, take on a life of their own. Ironically, it is often through creativity that you experience rebirth in a sense. As you begin to heal within, your inner work becomes outer work.

In *Walking on Water*, Madeleine L'Engle wrote, "I believe that each work of art, whether it is a work of great genius or something very small, comes to the artist and says, 'Here I am. Enflesh me. Give birth to me.' And the artist either willingly becomes the bearer of the work, or refuses."

Capture Your Ideas

Whenever I write, I first ask for spiritual guidance. Once the ideas start flowing, you must catch them. The more receptive you are to creative ideas, the more often they arrive. You may have noticed that the best ideas and inspirations come in moments of solitude. For me, they come in meditation, while I am getting ready for work, on my morning walk, in the shower or in the car, as well as when I am actively writing or speaking. And sometimes, ideas and inspirations arrive in my dreams. I keep notebooks everywhere so that I can record the ideas or inspirations as they come. Later, when I have more time, I develop them.

Although I put a lot of work, study and preparation into my lectures on spirituality, I rarely use notes or specifically prepare what I am going to say. This allows for spontaneous higher expression while I am lecturing. By letting God work through me in this way, I have found that the Higher Presence often provides more humor and profound inspiration than I could ever express alone.

Speaking Of Ideas ...

You may have great ideas, but do nothing with them because you think that they are not good enough. Understand that the ideas you receive are not *your* ideas, but rather God's ideas seeking to be expressed through you. The abundance and creativity of God extends into this world through you. With lack of trust in God, and in yourself, you limit this creative expression.

God Is Your Partner

You come into the fullest expression of your creativity when you remember that you are a co-creator with God. When you view God as a Divine partner, you move into living your life from the highest creative level. Once you partner with God, you become a co-creator in the ever evolving creation of the universe.

A man named Taylor had failed at several business ventures. He finally decided to make God his business partner, and then started a new business that he called "Lord & Taylor." He has been successful ever since.

It would be wonderful to have a partner who said, "I'll give you all the ideas you need, and the resources to implement them. All you have to do is receive the ideas and act on them." Well, you do have such a partner within you. Your partner is God. Ask for God's help and guidance in every aspect of your life.

Don't Limit Your Gifts

The problem for many of us is that we don't ask for help, and even when we do, we impose limitations in a multitude of ways. Such thoughts as, 'Well if I had his money or her degree or his talent or her spouse or his voice, Oh what I could do!' Nonsense! If you are not doing anything with the gifts and talents that are uniquely yours, you are not going to do anything with someone else's money, education or talent. You came here with your own gifts to extend. You were created to not only recognize your creative ability, but to own it and thus extend it.

A friend told me that she really enjoys painting and has a teacher who has confirmed her talent. Even so, she's doubtful. She asked me, "Is it always going to be like this, working at a job I hate rather than being able to support myself doing something I love?"

"Yes," I replied, "it's always going to be like that as long as you doubt your talent."

We say to the universe, "I think I have talent, but I don't think I'm good enough!" And in the next breath, "Gee, God, why can't I make any money with this talent?"

I gave someone one of my lecture tapes and told her she'd really like it. She looked at me as if I thought I was hot stuff or something. But what if I handed you one of my tapes and said,

"You really have to listen to this—but it's not that good!" Honoring your gifts is not prideful or arrogant, but humble. Refusing to acknowledge your God given gifts and talents is arrogant because in your refusal you are saying to God, "What you have given me is not good enough."

The belief that you are unworthy or have nothing to say keeps you from saying what you do have to say. In your refusal to create, you are not only hurting yourself, but all the people who could be served through your creations.

Invalidation Is Not Personal

You limit your creativity when you worry about what others will think or say. Have you noticed that there's always someone who will criticize you no matter what you do? Refrain from falling into the trap of people pleasing, or as Oprah calls it, "the disease to please." People pleasers are rarely happy because it is impossible to please everyone all the time.

In *The Artist's Way*, Julia Cameron coined the term "poisonous playmates." Poisonous playmates are those people who continually rain on your parade or stick a pin in the balloon of your vision. We have all known one and have probably been one. Parents, teachers, friends and acquaintances have been known to murder budding creativity at every turn. It helps to understand that these criticisms are not personal, but merely coming from one whose own creativity is blocked. Other people may not mean to burst your bubble, but do so because theirs is badly deflated.

When her first book was published, a friend told me that several family members totally ignored it. I said, "That's family crap!" It is sad, but true that those closest to you are often the ones who invalidate you the most. They may do so because their own creativity is blocked or because they choose to keep you in the role they have assigned to you. Nevertheless, I read somewhere that if you want to make your place in the sun, you have to quit sitting under the shade of the family tree.

I used to resent a particular friend because I felt she constantly invalidated me. I began to notice it wasn't just me she invalidated, but all of her friends when they achieved something in their lives. I brought this up to her and she replied with something quite interesting: "My brother jumps out of airplanes, and he doesn't understand why I don't validate that. But I have never jumped out of an airplane. I don't know what it's like." She equated the accomplishments of her friends to jumping out of an airplane and because she had not done it herself, she was unable to acknowledge it in anyone else. Invalidation and criticism from others is rarely personal. It's about them, not you. So don't use them to beat yourself up.

Go For the Joy!

In the movie "Mr. Holland's Opus," Mr. Holland offers to help one of his students after school with her clarinet practice. One afternoon she cries, "Everyone in my family is good at something. I just want to be good at something! I practice and practice but I'm just not good at this or anything else!"

"What do you like most about yourself?" asks Mr. Holland.

"My red hair because my father says it reminds him of a sunset."

"Okay," he replies, "you know the notes. They are in your mind and in your heart. Close your eyes and play the sunset." She did, and it was beautiful.

An overt focus on self, 'How will I look?' 'What will they say?' 'How will I be received?' will block creativity. You must give up attachment to what others will think or say, and create merely because it brings you joy. You write a book because it's in you. You sing a song because it's in you. You plant beautiful flowers because you must!

I once picked up a book that said, "Don't write a book until you have a publisher." I put it back on the shelf. Don't write a book because someone wants to publish it, write it because you must! If you feel compelled to say or do something as an extension of your spirit, then others will want to read it, hear it or see it. But whether they do or not, the doing of it brings you joy.

An Encounter with the Divine

I love this by Rumi:

> *In your light I learn how to love.*
> *In your beauty, how to make poems.*
> *You dance inside my chest,*
> *where no one sees you,*
> *but sometimes I do,*
> *and that sight becomes this art.*[28]

Rumi is speaking of an encounter with the Divine—collaboration with the Great Artist within. I never knew about my creative gifts until I encountered the Inner Presence.

Don't Suppress Your Gifts

You may be unaware that you have creative gifts to extend, even as your spirit yearns to express them. Suppression of this yearning can create emotional or physical dysfunction. In my practice, I have observed that some women have problems with their reproductive system, while others never do. Obviously, dysfunction in this area can occur for many reasons, but in my observation, the women who *chronically* exhibit this physical dysfunction are, on some level, unable to express themselves fully into the world. They may have sublimated their creative gifts for family, men or societal images, and then are unable to come forth with their own dreams, visions and desires. This can also be a factor with men who exhibit infertility problems, prostate dysfunction and the like.

A 43-year-old patient whose children were in college told me she wanted to have another baby. "You don't need another baby, you need a job!" I replied. She laughed and agreed that I was probably right. Consequently, she sought training to start a career, and is now thriving in that career. She said that it has brought new joy and purpose into her life. If you are over the age of forty, it is probably not another baby that is missing in your life, but the birth of your creative gifts.

Another woman I know raised six kids and in the process went back to school. By age fifty she had earned a black belt in karate, a Ph.D. in History, and is now a college professor. She told me if she had not done these things for herself, she would have gone stark-raving mad!

As a chiropractor, I treat patients with neck pain. I have frequently observed chronic (meaning, it's there all the time) neck pain in those who have not found an appropriate outlet for their emotions or creativity. Many of my patients who have chronic neck pain are unaware that they are actually seeking avenues of greater fulfillment in their lives. This physical pain is an indication that all is not right within.

Addiction and Creativity

Your addictions, compulsions and obsessions may also block your creativity. One of my patients began to compulsively spend money on expensive jewelry. She felt it had become an addiction. I referred her to a hypnotherapist who helped her alleviate it. A few years later, as a wedding gift, she gave me a beautiful painting she had painted herself. I asked her when she had started painting and she replied, "When you sent me to that hypnotherapist, she asked me under hypnosis what I would rather do than spend money on jewelry. I told her I wanted to paint." She had absolutely no idea that she wanted to do that. After that session, at the age of fifty-eight, she began taking painting classes and has proved to be very talented. More importantly, she loves it.

Beneath her compulsion to spend money was her need to create. That is probably true of all of our addictions, whether they be to substances, work, sex, relationships or whatever. Beneath your addictions lies your need to create. We live in an addictive society. Every one of us has some kind of addiction, even if it's being addicted to feeling not good enough. Liberation comes when you stop and ask, 'What is this addiction keeping me from doing with my life?'

You Are Not Too Old!

I once read that if you want to avoid Alzheimer's disease, create, and don't stop creating until you're dead. I have so many patients in their eighties and nineties who are as aware and acute as those much younger. I have noticed that the common denominator is that they love their life. They are active, they have friends, hobbies, and an interest in life. So many people think that they are too old. Too old for what? Too old to live your life to its fullest expression? You are never too old for that.

Your most substantial creativity is often expressed once you have gained enough maturity, wisdom and healing to extend it wisely. And as we know, maturity, wisdom and healing comes with experience and conscious awareness.

Paying Your Dues

In *The Sibling Society*, Robert Bly points out that a society that was formed and thrived on the work ethic now demands that we no longer be good at what we do through practice, discipline and perseverance, but merely famous, bathed in the warm glow of superficial attention. With no discipline required for genuine accomplishment, many young people are defeated before they even begin. He's right.

We currently live in a culture that worships youth, beauty, money and fame. When I was growing up, I received the message that true achievement and success is precipitated by years of practice, study and honing your craft (paying your dues). The people who we admire and respect are those who have done just that. You are here to practice and hone your talents, and through doing so you serve God, other people and your Self. If material rewards come out of your work—great! But even if they don't, you will still feel joy in the expression of your creative gifts because you will also, in some way, be serving others.

You Don't Need a Degree to Create

Your creative gifts emerge through living your life; often showing up in the area of your greatest interest. An area of greatest interest, however, may not be one you have a degree or training in. In retrospect, I can see that my area of greatest interest has always been in inspirational material. I don't have a degree in this and previously thought I had no talent in writing or public speaking. I received the training to do this work through the very living of my life.

Thomas Moore said, "Sometimes you have to put your work out into the world and let the work itself be your credentials." The creative process is an act of assertiveness. Through listening to and honoring the area you are most interested in, you may be brought to a level of service that you never dreamed possible.

The most unlikely people often do God's work. If you think about it, we are all the most unlikely in our mind because few of us feel good enough. I have often thought, 'Who am I to write a book about God?' I finally came to realize that I'm qualified to write this book because *I am* writing it.

In *Walking on Water*, Madeleine L'Engle points out, *when forced to accept your evident lack of qualification, there is no danger that you will confuse God's work with your own*. I am not likely to forget that this book was my spirit's idea, not mine. Nevertheless, I had to be willing to let God's ideas be expressed through me.

The only area of my life that flows perfectly is creativity because I don't get my hands into it other than to just do it. I recognize that my creativity comes from God, and I am fully aware that I cannot create without Divine help. Other areas of my life don't flow as easily because I think I can do it better by myself. I find it hard to believe, for example, that God knows as much about being a chiropractor as I do! Reflect on your life. Are there areas that do not flow as easily as they might because you are trying to do it all yourself? God desires to be expressed through you. Are you willing?

What Are You Yearning to Do?

Your yearnings come from your spirit, and your spirit is never wrong. Imagine what the world could be like if everyone did what they yearned to do. Imagine if everyone who yearned to feed the hungry did it. Imagine if everyone who yearned to write a book did it. Imagine if everyone who yearned to inspire others did it. What a different world we would live in. Instead, we often criticize those who are doing what we yearn to do. There is room for all of us because no one could do "it" exactly the way another could.

Extend the Beauty Within

Appreciating the creativity of others is also a creative act. I am not particularly visual, yet through my spiritual work I began to notice more beauty in the world. The truth is that if you don't see beauty in yourself, it's unlikely that you'll see it outside of you.

A woman who appears to be eighty or ninety fills our local

post office with the most beautiful flowers. She has been doing this on a weekly basis for many years without getting paid for it. She extends her beauty and joy in this way because it is something she wants to do.

You have beauty and joy to extend to the world. Do you doubt it? Do you doubt that you have inherent beauty to parade in the world? If you do, you are mistaken. God wills that you extend your beauty. There are so many ways you can bring beauty and meaning into the lives of others with your unique gifts.

Creative Blocks

Creative blocks come through trying to extend from the ego rather than your spirit. Using writer's block as an example, an author's first book more than likely came from the heart. After a certain amount of worldly success, or lack thereof, the ego speaks up and says, "You have to do *more*, you have to be *better*, you have to be the *best*! Or it says, "Give it up! You are not good enough!" If you are experiencing any kind of creative block, return to what compelled or inspired you to create in the first place. Chances are that it wasn't money, fame, or prestige but rather, it was something you felt you had to do. The expression of your creative gifts is like everything else in your life, it's a process. Your creativity gets better as you do.

Creativity Comes From Above

Being a chiropractor and a spiritual student and teacher, I have often thought about how spirituality and chiropractic work hand in hand. Chiropractic is based on the premise that only Divine Intelligence can heal. The purpose of the chiropractic treatment is to align the body with that Higher Intelligence. Spiritual chiropractic can be thought of as aligning our will with the will of God. It is God's will that you create!

Creativity, as well as health, comes from above, down, inside and out. From above to your mind, down to your heart, from inside of you to the outside world. All creativity comes from a mind linked with God, and once your heart grabs hold of it, you've really got something.

And so, as you go about your life, ask yourself the following questions: 'What do I yearn to do? What makes my heart sing?' Then, just do it!

HOW CAN I SERVE TODAY?

Before I began lecturing on spirituality, every day for several months I meditated on a particular prayer from *A Course in Miracles*:

> *Dear God,*
> *I am here only to be truly helpful.*
> *I am here to represent You who sent me.*
> *I do not have to worry about what to say or what*
> *to do, because You who sent me will direct me.*
> *I am content to be wherever You wish, knowing*
> *You go there with me.*
> *I will be healed as I let You teach me to heal.*[29]

It's powerful to remind yourself every day that you are here only to be helpful. And that no matter where you go, what you do or whom you meet, you have within you an ever present source of guidance and strength. If you are wondering what you are meant to do with the whole of your life, get off that and ask instead, "How can I be helpful today?"

Around the time that I prayed this prayer every day, I attended a meeting with a few people to talk about our businesses. At that time, I had been a chiropractor for ten years, studied spirituality for many years, and was passionately into *A Course in Miracles*. Prior to entering the meeting, I surrendered it and asked that God's will be done. Before long, I heard myself say that I knew I was meant to do something else with my life but didn't know what it was. A few minutes later I blurted out, "I am going to give lectures on spirituality." When I left the meeting and got into my car, I exclaimed, "You're going to do *what*?" One month later I did my first lecture, and on that day, I discovered a new level of passion, joy and service in my life.

It is important to note that previously I had no inclination to speak, let alone write about spirituality. Every day I asked how I could be helpful, and it all came about. Moreover, because I surrendered the aforementioned meeting to God, I feel that it was used to let me know what I was meant to do. So based on personal experience, when you acknowledge that you are here only to be helpful, stand back—you will soon find out how you can be.

Service Is an Attitude

To be helpful is to serve. And to serve is to be useful; to give of your Self to others. It is a universal law that you receive as you give. Through service, we acknowledge another's worth and our own. In this world, however, we are not taught that recognition of another's worth brings us to recognition of our own. Instead, we are taught to look out for number one. The primary focus is on what we can get in the form of money, status, love, possessions, validation, security, and so on, rather than on what we can give. We have been taught to embrace competition rather than cooperation—separation rather than communion. We cannot serve others this way. We serve others through recognition that we are all in this together.

After listening to a lecture on service, a participant said that she felt like service was just one more chore she had to do for God! Serving others does not involve doing something completely different than you do now. Service is an attitude. Service is doing whatever you are doing with an underlying recognition that it matters. You bring an attitude of meaning and service to your life when you realize that your only purpose is to be useful, and when you acknowledge that no task or person, including yourself, is insignificant. Live as if you make a difference in someone's life—you do.

Service extended with love is integral to living a meaningful life. Don't make the mistake of thinking that you have no way to serve. You need not wonder how you can serve next week, next year or a decade from now. Instead ask, "How can I serve today?" And then, as you go about your day—pay attention. Perhaps a person you are angry with enters your mind. You can serve him or her with a silent blessing of love and forgiveness. You can hold a door open for someone, listen to a friend in need or smile at a neighbor on your morning walk. Service need not be complicated.

Service on the Job
Work—embraced by some and despised by others, is a necessity for most of us. Bringing an attitude of service to the work you already do will enhance its meaning. The meaning you find in your work is in direct proportion to the meaning you are willing to give it. What makes work meaningful? The meaning is all too often placed on the work itself, associated with service orientated professions such as the healing arts, teaching or the ministry. But when you think about it, all work serves others in some way. All work makes a difference in someone's life. Whether you are raising children, flipping burgers, performing brain surgery, writing a book or painting a wall, your work is meaningful when you view it as a gift to someone else.

A friend told me of a teacher who shared that he wanted to find a way to serve humanity. He couldn't find anything that really touched him. My friend suggested, "Why don't you give back through thinking of your students as those whom you are meant to serve." He later said that as he applied this concept to his work, he enjoyed it so much more.

Someone else told me that when her boss asked her to type up college applications for his son. At first she was very angry about it. She then realized, "I can look at this in such a way that I'm helping him make the Great Escape!" Once she came to that conclusion, she was able to perform the task with love. You may be thinking, "Well, she shouldn't have had to do that!" True, but she did have to do it. We all have to do things we don't want to do—a lot of things. If you go to work with the attitude, "That's not my job!" is it any wonder that you have conflicts there?

Consider this: If you are an employer, think about what kind of employer you would want to have. Be that employer. If you are an employee, consider what kind of employee you would want working for you. Be that employee. If you have co-workers, ask yourself what kind of co-worker you would like to have working next to you. Be that co-worker.

I love what the philosopher Cicero said, "If you do only what is expected of you, you are a slave. But when you do more, you are free." Through your willingness to do more you fill up the space you are in. When you lovingly serve the person in front of you, other people and the universe take notice.

"But I Hate My Job!"

Over the years, I've interacted with many people who hate their job, dislike their co-workers, or feel underpaid and unappreciated. But then if they get fired or laid off, they're upset about it. This is understandable, of course. But if you've ever been fired or laid off from a job—was it from one you loved? Such an experience is often a gift because it forces you out of a job you probably needed to leave anyway. Many people who this has happened to are now doing something else they find more satisfying. Some people, however, choose to stay in a job they dislike. Such a choice is a lesson in and of itself.

You Are Here To Enjoy Your Life

Staying in a job that causes you anguish not only hurts you, but other people as well. There is another way you could serve that would bring more joy to yourself and others. However, you are not doing whatever that is if you are wasting your time at a job you hate. Not only does the job fill up your time, but it stirs up anger and resentment, and then you wonder why your life isn't more fulfilling.

Some people feel totally uninspired or stressed out in their jobs but they don't want to quit because of health insurance, retirement plans, vacation time or whatever. I have told a number of patients, "If you don't quit that job, you're going to need the health insurance, but you won't need the retirement plan."

If you are unwilling to move in a new direction, sometimes a crisis of one kind or another can push you into it. An illness or even chronic back pain can push you out of an unsatisfying job and into another that is more fulfilling. Many women who are forced to find jobs or careers because of divorce actually come into more fulfillment and independence in their lives. After a patient of mine who was trained as a medical assistant had cancer herself, she told me that she had decided to re-enter the work force to serve cancer patients because of the greater understanding and compassion she gained through her own experiences with the disease. Everything that has happened to you can be used to bring more meaning to your work, and thus to your life.

What Is A Calling?

A calling is frequently associated with a job or vocation. But we all have a calling. Each one of us is called to do something with and through our lives that will serve others and bring us joy. Your calling is a call from within. Your spirit yearns to express itself creatively, abundantly and with love. It whispers to you constantly about your calling in the form of inner yearnings and desires. When you listen to those yearnings and desires and heed them, you come into your calling.

You will know when you have found your calling. You will love it. You will feel joy when you do it. And it will be something that serves others. You are not here to suffer, sacrifice and be miserable, but to be happy. You are here to have fun. Many people flinch about that. "I'm here to have fun? I'm here to be happy? Are you kidding?" One might think, 'Isn't that selfish, Sheryl? Isn't it selfish to just serve in the ways that I love?' No, it's God's plan. How can you most serve others from a space of misery and unhappiness? Think about it.

An acquaintance was teaching spiritual classes and said to me, "I put all this work into it and not that many people come. I know that doesn't bother you, but I don't love it as much as you do."

"Then maybe you're not supposed to be doing that," I replied. I love giving spiritual lectures so much that I would give one to my dogs if they'd sit down and listen.

What Do You Love?

A clue may be found in answering the classic question: What would you do with your life if you knew you could not fail? If you could do anything you wanted to do, what would it be? Pause for a moment to write down what comes to mind.

Another clue may be found in reflecting on the things, people or ideas that inspire you. If you were to walk into a room and hear a conversation that you felt compelled to enter into, what would it be about? I'll bet you have thought of something haven't you?

Again, write it down. Your calling awaits only your recognition of it.

All Are Called

In his famous inaugural address, President John F. Kennedy urged, "Ask not what your country can do for you, but ask instead what you can do for your country." It's the same with God. It's not, "Dear God what can you do for me?" Rather, "Dear God, how can I express you?"

You may have heard that many are called and few are chosen. In truth, however, God calls everyone—very few of us call God back. Instead of answering God's call (the call of your spirit), what do you do instead? Do you put your spirit on hold (the cosmic call waiting) because you have a more important call? The more important call can be being too busy, refusal to spend time alone or a mind filled with fear, worry and anxiety. A patient told me that soon after she began to meditate, she heard, "put your TV in a box in the basement."

"Did you?" I asked.

We both laughed as she said, "yes." She explained that she had become obsessed with television. Please understand that there is nothing wrong with watching television, but she had been using it as a way to tune out the call of her spirit. In what ways are you tuning out the call of your spirit?

Return the Call

Today, pretend that you have a message from God: "Hi there. God calling. Can you do me a favor? I really need you to do something for me." In your mind, return the call, 'Dear God, I received your message. I don't know what you want me to do, but I want you to know that I'm willing and available.'

Answering God's call doesn't require time, money or

resources. The only qualification is willingness. Nevertheless, you may not want to answer God's call due to fear that you might be asked to do something that you won't want to do.

In *Windows of the Soul*, Ken Gire reflected on his own feelings: "I feared that if I got too serious about my relationship with God, that if I got close enough to where He could see the whites of my eyes, He might call me out from the crowd, call me by name, send me somewhere I didn't want to go." And later, once he discovered his passion for writing, he wondered, "Could something that made me feel this good, this fulfilled, this whole, be God calling?" Yes!

The Tao Te Ching answers, *In work, do what you enjoy.*

Man is not born to solve the problems of the universe, but to find out what he has to do, answers Goethe.

Katharine Graham answers, *To love what you do and to feel that it matters—how could anything be more fun*!

And finally, Jenifer Levin, in her novel *The Sea of Light*, answers, *Whatever we put our most into, like our time, and sweat and blood, well that is the thing we make our own. Because after a while it smells like us, it tastes like us. After a while it calls out our name.*

There is something you are meant to do that no one else can do exactly the way you can. If you don't do it it's lost to the world. Don't make the mistake of thinking that it has to be a big thing. It may be, or it might simply involve your job, your hobbies, volunteer work, or your parenting. My sister is an awesome stay-at-home mom. I marvel at her. I could not do what she does, nor could she do what I do. And that's the point. You are meant to do something unique to you that will serve others and bring you joy.

Life Leads You to Your Calling

You will most likely discover your calling through the living of your life. Corrie ten Boom demonstrates this in her book, *The Hiding Place*. Corrie and her sister, Betsie, were Christian women who hid Jews in their attic during the Nazi invasion and occupation of Holland. They were captured and sent to concentration camps. The book is Corrie's story of that period of their lives.

While in prison, Corrie saw the saintliness of her sister, Betsie: "It was almost as if she didn't mind being there." Betsie served the other prisoners through teaching the Bible which had to be sneaked into the prison. At one point the prisoners were moved to an area of the prison that had a lot of fleas. When Corrie complained about the fleas, Betsie replied, "Everything happens for a reason, we thank God even for the fleas." It was later revealed that Betsie was able to teach the Bible without persecution because the guards never came to that area of the prison. Why? The fleas! Even they served a purpose.

One day Betsie said to Corrie, "When this is over, we must take care of these people, we must love them, we must show them that love is greater." It wasn't until later in the day that Corrie realized that Betsie had been talking about the guards, not the prisoners. "When I looked at the guards, I saw a gray uniform," wrote Corrie. "Betsie, however, saw a wounded human being."

Betsie died in prison. On her deathbed she whispered to Corrie, "You must tell people. You must tell people." When Corrie was finally released from prison and returned home, she was haunted by, *You must tell people.* In the latter half of her life she began to lecture and write on their experiences. But prior to even hiding the Jews, Corrie had asked God, "How can I help these people?" Her calling stemmed from that question.

I read that book and others like it in my early years of spiritual practice and became incredibly inspired to serve. But my ego seductively broke in, 'Now, Sheryl, do you really want to serve God? I mean, come on. Do you really want to end up in India teaching spiritual principles? Do you want to end up in some prison ministering to all the people there? Let's get serious about this God thing. How much do you want to get into this?'

'Good point,' I thought. 'If *that* is what I have to do in order to serve God, thank you, I will pass!' But then the Holy Spirit broke through, 'Sheryl, you too can serve in a powerful way. The people you touch in your daily life need love just as much as people any place else.'

'An even better point!'

You Can't Be All Things to All People

When it comes to serving in the world you may think, "Okay, tomorrow morning, I am going to call the Salvation Army, or I am going to feed the homeless, or I am going to give money to charity." All great things to do, but true service is giving through your heart. If you are doing certain things because you think you should that is fine, but not nearly as effective as doing such things because you feel joy when you do them. If you are doing for others only to get a paycheck, a pat on the back or a wink from God, you are not serving them. You most serve others as you extend from your heart to theirs.

It is important to understand that you cannot be all things to all people. Don't try to be. It will make you crazy! Serve in the ways that you love. There are many avenues of service where I have no gifts, and no interest. I no longer condemn myself for that. I love studying and teaching spirituality. I love helping people gain a new vision for their lives. So that's what I do.

All Will Be Provided

We would really love to do this or that, but think that we don't have the time, resources, money or whatever. All that is needed, remember, is your willingness. Speaking of money … At some point along the way, I came to the realization that I wanted money to come as an extension of my spirituality rather than from the exclusion of it. This is not the fast track to money, although it is the rewarding one.

As I focused on my inner healing rather than trying to get more from the world, I found that everything I needed came when I needed it: Time, money, opportunities, inner strength—not to mention editors and a publisher. This does not mean, however, that your needs will be met in the way or in the time frame of your expectations. From the day I began to seriously seek a publisher for this book it took two years, to the day, to acquire one. There were moments during those years when I felt disheartened at the prospect of ever getting my work out into the world.

Ironically, while editing this portion of the book I had a revelation that turned things around for me. After doing some additional editing here, the next day I heard the Inner Voice say, 'So Sheryl, in your book you've written that everything came when you needed it. Perhaps you should edit it to say that you were provided with everything you needed, *but* a publisher.' Upon hearing this I laughed out loud and thought, 'Yes, God will provide everything I need—but a publisher? Can't do that!' Along with this realization, one week later came a publisher.

In retrospect, I see how necessary those additional two years were to not only the growth of this book, but to my inner growth as well. And so, based on even more experience, I know that when God calls and you answer, all that you need *will* be provided. All will be provided in God's way and timing—not yours.

"How Can I Serve Today?"

Are you willing to return God's call today? If so, then you need to spend some time with God today. But that need not be more than one minute. In your willingness to be silent and alone for a minute, you essentially say to God, "Here I am. I'm giving you what I have." During that minute you can say, "Dear God, Sheryl told me you left a message. I'm just calling you back. How can I serve today?" Something as simple as that, done every day, could change your entire life. And then once you are willing to spend one minute with God, you will move into spending more time as your desire for that Presence expands. Your life will change as you allow yourself to hear the call of your spirit.

Ask to be used by God. 'Dear God, I am willing to be your instrument. May You give me the opportunity to live Your light, to extend Your love in the way that You would have me extend it.' It's not about being famous, a hero, or a world leader, it's about serving in your corner of the universe. It's about recognizing that your life is filled with meaning and purpose exemplified by your very existence. It is about acknowledging that no task is unimportant, no job insignificant and no person unworthy.

And so, as you go about your life, remember that you are called to extend God's love. You are called to extend God's forgiveness. You are called to extend the Divine in a way unique to you. It is a mighty call. Ask for the willingness to answer that call today.

PREGNANT WITH POSSIBILITY

As you enter yet another new day, may you become pregnant with the possibility that something new can be born within you. You are not given tomorrow. You are given today. What will you do with it? How will you respond?

Within you is the possibility of a life lived with happiness, peace and purpose. Within you is the possibility that you can creatively serve others in ways that extend your love. This is God's vision for you. Decide today to accept that vision so that you can bring your divine possibilities into the light of reality.

When we think about a new vision for our lives it usually has to do with our bodies, financial situations, relationships or our jobs. But before we see change on the outside, we must first seek to change within.

The process of delivering possibility into reality is analogous to childbearing. The physical birth process is wondrous and mysterious, but no more or less so than giving birth to your Divine possibilities. But first, can you even conceive of the possibility that you can change your life? If so, then you can become pregnant with this possibility and ultimately give birth to it.

Conception

To "conceive" means "to become pregnant with; to begin something new." In this stage, you become receptive to God's vision for your life. You become pregnant with possibility. A possibility is that which may occur if not hindered by serious obstacles. The greatest obstacles are preconceived notions of what your possibilities are. In other words, instead of aligning with God's vision for your life, you may focus on what you think you want. You might think that fulfillment will come through opening a business, writing a book, having a child, (insert your own). It's not that you cannot have what you think you want. God gives you your desires—they are clues to your joy. When you bring God into the process of delivering your possibilities into reality, you will find more satisfaction as you move into that desire, or you will find that God has a better plan for your life.

In the previous chapter on service I shared how I began speaking and writing on spirituality. When I asked, "How can I serve?" I had no idea that it would manifest into teaching spirituality. First, I cultivated a relationship with God. Then I asked, "How can I serve?" And now, you hold this book in your hands.

If you could get off focusing on what you think you want, and instead focus on how you can creatively serve others in ways that extend your love, only God knows where that could lead and how it will manifest in your life.

God has a vision for you that will bring you joy. The Inner Presence will not only communicate to you what it is, but will also give you the strength to do what it requires, and to succeed in all that is related to it. In order to hear this guidance, however, you must nurture a relationship with the God within.

Flirtation or Relationship?

A relationship begins with courtship. As you initiate a courtship with God, you might begin with flirtation. Most of us get into God to fix something in our lives. But as our relationship with the Divine deepens, we come to recognize that there is so much more. We will not be able to carry our possibilities from conception to delivery if we don't get past the flirtation stage of the relationship. If we trifle or toy with the idea of God, we will not allow this Presence to become an active reality in our lives.

Flirtation does not mean that you are ready for a committed relationship, much less a pregnancy! Flirtation may evolve into a love affair, but then the love affair is also very different from a committed relationship. The love affair is the fun part. It's new and exciting and can lead to other possibilities. To deliver possibility into reality, however, you must develop a committed relationship because you will need all the love, wisdom, guidance and strength that only the Inner Presence can provide.

If you want to deepen a relationship with someone you must listen to, spend time with, and seek him or her. It's the same with God. The fruits that evolve from such an intimate relationship are not experienced until you evolve into a deeper level of commitment. Review the previous chapters on prayer and meditation because they will help you in this initial stage of learning to become more receptive to inner guidance.

Once you begin to flirt with prayer and meditation, you essentially say to the universe, "I am willing to try something new." A helpful prayer: 'Dear God, how do you desire to express your love and creativity through me?' The universe will respond immediately to your slightest invitation. You will be guided to the ideas, information, people or whatever is needed that will lead you further along your path. You may also want to review the chapters on creativity and service because they lay down ideas that are helpful to becoming pregnant with something new in your life.

STAGE TWO

♾

Pregnancy

You have conceived of a vision and now you are pregnant with it. The pregnancy stage is a preparation period. To deliver a possibility into a reality, you need preparation. You must move into a higher level of spiritual maturity. During this process, you are being prepared to allow God to be expressed through you.

We often want to skip the preparation stage and get on with having a realized vision. But it doesn't work that way. In fact, that cannot work because we must embody the qualities and the character that are necessary to deliver a possibility into a reality. In this stage the real work begins.

The process of carrying possibilities through full term will be one of the most important, and also one of the most difficult things you ever do. This process will challenge you. It will bring up fear, doubt and insecurity. You will face tests and trials. Don't run from or seek to avoid them. You won't gain by running away from your challenges. You will gain much, however, from going through them and letting them teach you what you need to learn. As you meet these challenges with God, you will begin to develop faith and trust in the benevolence of the universe. It is a process that will evolve slowly, taking more time than a mere nine months. But the slowness is part of the plan.

Anyone who brings new vision to others had to go through a preparation period—even Jesus. We don't know much about Jesus' life until he began his public ministry at age 30. So what was he doing until then? The Bible gives us a clue when it says, *he grew.*[30] Just like the rest of us he, too, had to mature in body, mind and spirit before he could deliver his possibility into reality. This process takes time and occurs in stages.

In the initial stages of pregnancy, you don't look pregnant. No one else can tell. You must sometimes carry a possibility on the inside for a long time before it becomes visible on the outside. Before I did my first lecture on spirituality I had to spend many years preparing to do so. Those years involved a lot of inner excavation. I had to dig down to bare my negative patterns so that they could be exposed to the healing light.

My only desire was to heal. I assumed that the outcome would be that all my problems would be gone. Not so. Some of my problems became worse than ever. I had come to a level of peace within my problems and that's when I realized that this God stuff works! I had no idea that my desire to heal my negative patterns would evolve into teaching spirituality. When that possibility became a reality, people who had known me for years said, "Where did that come from?"

When you are willing to burrow deep within yourself and bring forth what you find to the light, you transform. I can see why people were surprised by my transformation because my inner work was not something I talked about with others. It was between God and me. To see changes in your life, you must first seek to change within. Many inner changes will take place as you travail through this period.

Does It Still Fit?

When a woman is pregnant her body expands so that she can become a large enough vessel to deliver new life. During this expansion phase her former clothes no longer fit. Symbolically, you too must stop wearing that which no longer fits.

To embody the character and qualities necessary to bring

possibilities into reality, you must pay attention to those patterns of resentment, guilt, self-pity and fear that no longer fit your highest expression. You must also look at your attitudes, values and beliefs, and then evaluate whether or not they still serve you. Reviewing all the previous chapters will be a helpful exercise because they not only point to the ways you have been choosing against higher purpose in your life, they will also guide you in a new direction.

You Must Stand Alone

Even in a physical pregnancy, a woman stands alone. Yes, she may have the support of a mate or other people, but only she can go through the birth process. Although you have received a new vision for your life, it's likely that God didn't tell your family, friends and acquaintances about it. So rather than encourage you, other people may talk about, criticize or be discouraging. Anyone who does anything in this world goes through this. Don't let the judgment and criticism from others hold you back. Carry your vision close to your heart. When you are called, be willing to stand up and say, "Yes!" In truth, you are never alone. As you develop a committed relationship with God, you will realize that you have ever present guidance, comfort and strength.

You Need Other People

You must stand alone. But paradoxically, you will need other people to deliver your possibilities into realities. John Donne said that no man is an island. We need each other. Be on notice that everyone you meet is important. What you do with that encounter, however, is up to you. It baffles me how many people were needed to get this book into your hands. I could not possibly recount everyone who contributed to it in some way. It's like spiritual midwifery—so many other people are instrumental to the delivery of your vision. While they are serving you, you are serving them as well.

Don't Give Up!

The purpose of the preparation period is to bring you to a level of spiritual and emotional maturity that is required for the delivery of your vision. Along the way you will be challenged and tested. If you fearfully succumb to these experiences rather than seeking to use them for growth and healing, you might stop at an early stage.

God has a vision to extend to this world, and you are necessary for the fulfillment of it. What God is expressing through me with this book could not be expressed without me. And whatever God desires to express through you couldn't be expressed without you. When you don't go through the preparation process, you aren't just hurting yourself, you not only guarantee that you'll live an unfulfilled life, but you deprive the people that could benefit from your unique gifts and talents. God loses your part in the plan because no one else can extend it the same way you can. Let's look at some of the ways that we can halt our progress.

It's Too Hard!

Frequently, we look at the lives of others and say, "I want that!" We are seeing their realized possibility. We may want what other people have, but probably have no idea what they went through to get it. And if we did, we just might not want to do it because it's too hard!

I read a book that premised the idea that working on yourself doesn't work. In it, the authors recounted the various experiences they had over the years that led them to the discovery that transformation is easy. They now give weekend seminars on how one can be transformed instantaneously. But the authors discounted an important part of the process: It took numerous years and various experiences to get to a point where they realized that transformation is easy. And just like them, we too, must journey through the experiences of our lives to glean this truth. In truth, transformation may be easy, but it's going to take longer than a weekend.

If you've read the previous chapters, you know that working on yourself is not about fixing yourself. Instead, it is a life-long process of removing the barriers to the remembrance that you already are complete. We live in a culture that wants everything fast and easy. We want our spiritual growth to be that way as well. But it doesn't happen like that. Working on yourself doesn't work if you think that it involves effecting change from the outside. Transformation must first start within. The pregnancy process is a transformation process. You cannot give birth to a baby instantaneously. The birth of your vision cannot occur that way either.

Throughout this book I have used the term "inner work." For many, work denotes labor and toil of one kind or another. But work can also mean effort directed to accomplish something. Inner work is the work of disciplining and training your mind so that you can not only become aware of your thoughts and their effects in your life, but so that you can direct your thoughts to accomplish something. This inner work is a requirement to realizing your vision. And yes, it is hard work. But it's not too hard. What's too hard is living a life in despair. What's too hard is living life as a victim. What's too hard is living life angry, resentful, and feeling not good enough.

Is It God's Plan Or Yours?

You might think that it's too hard because you are attempting to carry out your plan or someone else's plan for your life, instead of God's plan. One way you can tell that it's not God's plan is if you are frequently frustrated, dazed, crazed and confused.

If it's God's plan, you will feel joy and passion as you go

through the process, even with its roadblocks here and there. But we often don't want to do the many small things that lead us to the big things in life. Many tedious details go along with carrying your vision. As you prepare to give birth to your possibilities, however, you will be given the grace to do the tedious and difficult things.

If you want to make God laugh, tell him your plans. You don't have to add anything to God's plan but to receive it, you must be willing to let go of your own. Hanging onto expectations of how life should be, rather than opening up to what it could be, is what screws you up. What it could be—is so much fun!

You Don't Get To See the Big Picture

You can give up on your possibilities if you are afraid to try something new because you don't know how it will turn out in advance. Well, I know something about this. In my experience, guidance comes incrementally. Several years ago, if someone had told me that I would some day speak and write on spirituality, not only would I have thought they were nuts, it would have scared me to death! 'Me? Talk about God? I don't think so!' I would not have wanted to do it, and probably would have blocked it. Yet nothing else has brought me more joy.

The guidance I received from the day I did my first lecture on spirituality to the publishing of this book came in increments that were sometimes years apart. Act on the guidance you receive today. Don't be afraid that you will be asked to do something you won't want to do. You will be asked to do something that you will love to do. Take the risk and trust that God will reveal a new plan to you, and that you will love it.

Several years ago a friend's house burned to the ground. Everything they owned was lost, including the start up inventory for a new business. Almost immediately afterward they knew it was a new beginning for them. They bought a motor home and decided to travel around the country. At the time of this writing they have been on the road for eight years. They have a website, www.roadtripamerica.com; and have been featured in *People* magazine. Megan Edwards published a book about their travels, *Roads from the Ashes*. But what if God had said, "First, your house will burn to the ground. Then you will live in a motor home for a few years. And then, you will write a book about your experiences." Do you think they would have gone for it? No way! That's probably one reason why we don't get to see the big picture—we probably wouldn't want to do it. But would they give up those experiences now? No way!

There are many experiences that we'd like to bypass in this lifetime, and our home burning down is one of them. Nevertheless, we all go through painful things that we don't understand. Such crisis experiences may tempt us to give up. But if you could come to trust that whatever you go through is a necessary preparatory experience to lead you to serving at a higher level and with more joy, such a realization does make the going through it easier. It carries with it a sense that your life has profound meaning and purpose. This is why it is so important to nurture a relationship with the Inner Presence. With God, you can go through anything and come out of it victorious. So before you give up on your vision, turn to God.

Yes, You Will Be Rejected

Over the years, I wrote two previous books and sent them out to publishers and agents. I received countless rejections. I now recognize that those books were not publishable, and that they were actually practice versions of this one. I once asked God, "Well if those books weren't meant to be published anyway, why did I have to go through the process of writing them and sending them out?" The answer I received was that I had to be tested to see if I was going to let the value of my work and the value of my worth rest on rejection letters. In addition to that, I had to learn how to write! Those previous books and rejection letters were just part of the process of growth and preparation needed to impart this one. Even so, I have a pile of rejections for this book too—*Never Give Up!*

I used an obvious example of rejection, but there are many ways that our fears of rejection can hold us back. Rejection is part of the deal. With the publishing of this book, I might receive hundreds, perhaps thousands of letters from people telling me I'm "wrong." So what. It's part of the deal. If you cannot handle rejection, you will most likely lose your vision. The previous chapters, "I Am Good Enough!" and Conscious Creativity address this. Go back and read those chapters, and then bring awareness to where this fear of rejection might be alive and well in your life. Never forget that the only person who can abolish your vision is you.

"But I'm Afraid"

Aren't we all? Anyone who has brought his or her vision from conception to delivery did so, at least initially, in fear. No one on this planet popped out of the womb with the knowledge that they had what it takes. Whether or not you think you have what it takes, there is a Presence within you that will enable you to fulfill any task you've been asked to do. You didn't find your vision, your vision found you. If you've accepted it, then, with God, you have what it takes to deliver it.

Fear can paralyze you and cause you to deny your vision. When you have been hurt, betrayed or rejected, you might fear it happening again, succumb to such fears, and thus give up. If you have been hurt in relationships, you may have decided to give up on dating, or interacting with other people. You must confront the fear in order to learn that it has no power over you. Talk to your fear. Ask it what it is attempting to teach you.

The night before I did my first lecture on spirituality, I was almost paralyzed by fear. I prayed about it and opened *A Course in Miracles* to this: *Do not be concerned with your own readiness, but have consistent trust in mine.*[31] That was a Divine message for me. The Holy Spirit was essentially saying to me, "You don't have to be ready, just trust that I am." If due to fear I had not done that first lecture, I would not have experienced the joy and healing I've gained from doing them; I would not have had such an opportunity to serve others, and you would not be reading this book.

If you do the one thing you're afraid of, you will find that it brings forth so many other experiences and opportunities. The people who are living happy and purposeful lives are those who are out on a limb saying, "Okay God, I'm out here! You told me you'd be here too!"

Faith and Trust

The process teaches us to have faith and trust in God. You learn to have faith and trust in God when you turn to that Presence time and time again within every facet of your life. Faith and trust are integral to having a committed relationship with God just as it is for any other relationship.

Please understand that it takes just as much faith and trust to do something you love, to deliver possibility into reality, as it does to go through a crisis. In fact, it often takes more because in our world, we get a lot more support in crisis and suffering than we do in pursuit of something we love. If you were to say to your friends "I'm working on being a more loving person, or I'm going to be successful" or "I'm going to make my dreams come true," very few people, if any, will respond with, "Rah! Rah!" Don't lose heart because other people don't support you. Have faith and trust in the Presence within that is your power, your strength and your Divine Cheerleader.

Keep your vision in sight at all times. On conception you attain a vision, but you don't know how long it will take to come into fulfillment. You don't know what you will have to go through. You are not given the specifics of how, what and when. To navigate through the how, what and when, you must carry your vision in your heart and trust God for the rest. Appreciate all that occurs in the process. Recognize that all experiences can be used by God to bring forth blessings in your life. Faith and trust in God will keep you from giving up.

It's Taking Too Long!

When "It's taking too long!" you can become discouraged and stop at an early stage. The preparation required to give birth to your vision takes time. It's going to take longer than a few weeks, months or even years. Living a joyous life doesn't occur on delivery. You experience joy when you begin to see the gifts, purpose and meaning inherent in every single day of your life.

You have probably heard that it's the journey that is important, not the destination. Well it's true. Perhaps it would have been easier if I had been told at the start of many of my symbolic pregnancies that it would take years, not months. But I needed years, not months! And so do you. The lessons learned and the spiritual maturity attained during those years, are necessary to not only realize your vision, but to also live it in the years to come.

In *The Message*, Eugene Peterson expresses the process:
All around us we observe a pregnant creation. The difficult times of pain throughout the world are simply birth pangs. But it's not only around us; it's within us. The spirit of God is arousing us within. We are also feeling the birth pangs. These sterile and barren bodies of ours are yearning for full deliverance. That is why waiting does not diminish us, any more than waiting diminishes a pregnant mother. We are

enlarged in the waiting. We, of course, don't see what is enlarging us. But the longer we wait the larger we become and the more joyful our expectancy.

Meanwhile, the moment we get tired in the waiting, God's Spirit is right alongside helping us along. If we don't know how or what to pray, it doesn't matter. He does our praying in and for us, making prayers out of our wordless sighs, our aching groans. He knows us far better than we know ourselves, knows our pregnant condition, and keeps us present before God. This is why we can be so sure that every detail in our lives is worked into something good.[32]

You must come to recognize that every experience on your journey is necessary and can be worked into something good. Just because it's taking too long, don't give up on your vision.

Premature Birth

We want it to happen—now! Understand that it's the ego that wants "it" to happen now, not your spirit. The Bible says that the vision is for an appointed time and hastens to fulfillment. If it seems slow in coming, wait—it's on its way. It's not up for you to know the time or the date, that's up to God. But be assured that you will have power and ability from the Spirit within.[33]

If you try to give birth to something before you are ready, you just might blow it. God's timing is perfect. In our impatience, however, we may try to force the outcome before we have completed the preparation period. Don't do this. Trials and difficulties test your faith and help you develop perseverance. When you attempt to get out of things prematurely, you don't fully mature, and are thus incapable of going on.

Labor

During spiritual pregnancy your vision, just like a baby, takes on a life of its own. It kicks and moves around. It lets you know that there is something within that yearns to come out. You not only have a vision, but your vision has you.

Throughout your pregnancy you have been preparing for labor. Is it going to be painful? You bet! Labor involves pain. Some people will never give birth to anything in their lives because they want to avoid pain. But would you rather go through the pain of giving birth to your vision or instead, labor under the burden of living a life devoid of passion, purpose, meaning and joy?

The process is the same whether you are giving birth to a child, a book, a career, or a new you. Carl Jung said that there is no birth in consciousness without pain. When a woman gives birth to a baby, she often forgets how painful it was. Although I haven't given birth to a real baby, I've experienced tremendous emotional pain and darkness during my years of spiritual growth and preparation. But from where I stand today, I don't remember the pain and the dark nights because through learning to navigate through the dark with God, I came into the light. I no longer remember what the pain felt like because I am not stuck in it anymore.

Transition

In the labor stage possibility begins to move into reality. Here, we go through a transition period. The Bible tells us that the way is narrow and constricted by pressure, but it is the narrow path that leads to life.[34] Few follow this narrow path for it demands that they be contracted by pressure so that they might expand to live a full life. Here we are told to—push! And when the pressure becomes so great and we think we cannot continue, we are told, again—push!

The baby comes when it is due. You will move on to delivery if you do not lose heart, grow weary or give up. When close to delivery of your vision, you will want to give up. But you must move forward. You will grow weary, but you cannot give up if you want to live a powerful and fulfilling life. Trust God's timing.

I experienced this as I was finishing this book. I was finally in the labor stage and it was then that I thought, 'Enough already! I've had enough of this. I want to quit!' I heard the Inner Voice say, 'That is not an option.' I laughed because I wasn't going to give up anyway. I had come too far. I couldn't turn back at that point. I had to push and give birth to this baby. During this period I thought of the Holy Spirit as my Divine Lamaze coach, holding my hand and guiding me through the narrow gate.

If you don't think that the process should be difficult, then it is going to be equally difficult for you to bear down and give birth to what God desires that you give birth to. Let's face it, life is often difficult. But good will come out of all difficulties if you are willing to bear down and let them bring you to a higher level of spiritual maturity.

God Is Your Partner

God is on your side. *God is a partner in your labor.*[35] In a partnership, each partner must be willing to do their part. You need to cooperate with the Inner Presence knowing that when you do your part, only then can God work in and through you. Your part is not to give up on your vision, give it a premature birth or give up your faith.

Over the years, I have come to the most amazing discovery— God is not a silent partner. We are guided constantly. The problem is that we're usually not listening. As you develop a deep relationship with God, you will begin to listen more often, and you too will be amazed by this truth.

STAGE FOUR

࿊

Delivery

It's not your job to deliver your vision into the world. Your job is to *prepare* to deliver it. In his fabulous book, *The Soloist*, Mark Salzman writes: *You cannot make great music happen; you can only prepare yourself for it to happen. To a degree, your preparation determines what will happen, but once it starts happening you have to surrender yourself to it.*

You have traversed through pregnancy. You have not denied your vision or given it a premature birth. What you gain through the process will determine what can happen. But once in labor, you must surrender to letting God be God in your life.

You receive your vision from God, go through the birth process and thus something new comes out of your union. This is what happens during the birth of a child in reality and symbolically—two create something new.

Determine today that no matter what, you are going to make it to the delivery date and beyond. Trust God. And in due time you will reap a harvest. The baby comes when it is due and not a moment before. Your vision is delivered when you are prepared and mature enough to nurture it into all that it can be.

Possibility Becomes Reality

You aren't done once you deliver. Giving birth to your vision involves great responsibility—a changed life. Your vision will continue to demand your attention. It will need to be fed and attended to. But you won't mind because you will love it.

As you go about your life,
become pregnant with the possibility
that something new can be born within you.
Seek God's plan for your life, today.

ABOUT THE AUTHOR

Dr. Sheryl Moore Valentine has studied spirituality for over twenty years—and has lectured on spiritual principles since 1993. She is a doctor of chiropractic, practicing in southern California since 1985.

To order recordings of her live lectures on spirituality, please visit www.SherylValentine.com

NOTES ON REFERENCES

All definitions found in this book are from *Random House Webster's College Dictionary* unless otherwise noted.

Citations attributed to *A Course in Miracles* are keyed to the 2nd edition. Examples are as follows:

T-4.III.2:2	– Text, chapter 4, section 3, paragraph 2, sentence 2.
WB-L25.3:4	– Workbook, lesson 25, paragraph 3, sentence 4.
M-4.3:2	– Manual, question 4, paragraph 3, sentence 2.
C-6.4:2	– Clarification of Terms, term 6, paragraph 4, sentence 2.
S-1.I.1:7	– The Song of Prayer, chapter 1, section 1, paragraph 1, sentence 7.

Citations attributed to the Bible are footnoted with standard usage: Matthew 2:4—The book of Matthew, chapter 2, verse 4.

FOOTNOTES

1   ACIM, T-16.IV.6:1

2   ACIM, T-18.V.7:3-6 paraphrased

3   ACIM, WB-L192..2:3

4   ACIM, T-15.XI.10:5

5   Compassion and Forgiveness, audio by Sanaya Roman

6   Unknown—paraphrase by Sheryl Valentine

7   ACIM, T-29.VII.1:9, T-30.I.10:2

8   The three quotes on this page are from Matthew 7:3, 5:44 and 5:38 (*The Message*) respectively.

9   Unknown—paraphrased by Sheryl Valentine

10 From *There's A Hole In My Sidewalk*, by Portia Nelson

11 ACIM, T-31.VIII.3:2

12 *The Edgar Cayce Handbook for Creating Your Future*, by Mark Thurston, Ph.D. and Christopher Fazel.

13 Mark 11:24-25 *Amplified Bible*

14 Jacob A. Riss—Writer, Social Activist 1901

15 ACIM, T-5.VII.5:1,6:1

16 ACIM, T-3.VI. 3:1

17 Revelation 3:20

18 ACIM, S-1.III.2:4

19 ACIM, WB-ep.6:7

20 Written in collaboration with Michael Paul Harcourt

21 Based on "The Prodigal Son," Luke 15:11, ACIM.T-8.VI.4:1-4

22 Isaiah 61:10

23 ACIM, WB-L182

24 Fuller, Thesaurus of Anecdotes

25 Carl Jung

26 The story as it appears here is part paraphrase and part original inspiration—inspired by L. Frank Baum's, *The Wizard of Oz.*

27 Inspired by Gregory Maguire's *Wicked, The Life and Times of the Wicked Witch of the West*

28 From *The Essential Rumi*, translated by Coleman Barks

29 ACIM, T-2.V.18:1

30 AB, NASB, Luke 2:40

31 ACIM, T-2.V.4:2

32 *The Message*, Romans 8:22

33 Habakkuk 2:2-3, Acts 1:6, Romans 8:28

OTHER WHITE KNIGHT BOOKS

Adoption	A Swim Against The Tide, *David R.I. McKinstry*
Biography	The Life and Times of Nancy Ford-Inman, *Nancy Erb Kee*
Education	From Student to Citizen, *Prof. Peter Hennessy*
Health	Prescription for Patience, *Dr. Kevin J Leonard* Brain Injury, *Alan J. Cooper*
Humour	*By David R.I. McKinstry:* • An Innkeeper's Discretion BOOK ONE • An Innkeeper's Discretion BOOK TWO Will That Be Cash or 'Cuffs?, *Yvonne Blackwood*
Inspiration	"Oh My God. It's ME!", *Dr. Sheryl Valentine* *By Rev. Dr. John S. Niles:* • The Art of Sacred Parenting • How I Became Father to 1000 Children *By Darlene Montgomery:* • Conscious Women, Conscious Lives ONE • Conscious Women, Conscious Lives TWO • Conscious Women, Conscious Careers Happiness: Use It or Lose It, *Rev. Dr. David "Doc" Loomis* Sharing MS (Multiple Sclerosis), *Linda Ironside* Sue Kenney's My Camino, *Sue Kenney*
Personal Finances	Don't Borrow $Money$, *Paul E Counter*
Poetry	Loveplay, *Joe Fromstein and Linda Stitt* Two Voices, A Circle of Love, *Serena Williamson Andrew*
Politics & History	Prophets of Violence, Prophets of Peace, *Dr. K. Sohail* Turning Points, *Ray Argyle*
Self-Help	*By Dr. K. Sohail* • The Art of Living in Your Green Zone • The Art of Loving in Your Green Zone, • The Art of Working in Your Green Zone, *with Bette Davis* • Love, Sex and Marriage, *with Bette Davis*
True Crime – Police	"10-45" Spells Death, *Kathy McCormack Carter* Life on Homicide, *Former Police Chief Bill McCormack* The Myth of The Chosen One, *Dr. K. Sohail*

Visit our website www.whiteknightbooks.ca or request catalogue.

RECOMMENDED READING FROM OTHER PUBLISHERS

History	An Amicable Friendship (Canadiana), *Jan Th. J. Krijff* Pro Deo, *Prof. Ronald Morton Smith*
Religion	From Islam to Secular Humanism, *Dr. K. Sohail*
Biography	Gabriel's Dragon, *Arch Priest Fr. Antony Gabriel*